W9-AEA-977

Billboard®

TOP 1000 SINGLES
1955-1992

Hal Leonard Publishing Corporation

7777 West Bluemound Road P.O. Box 13819 Milwaukee, WI 53213

Hal Leonard Publishing Corporation
7777 West Bluemound Road P.O. Box 13819 Milwaukee, WI 53213

CONTENTS

A listing of the *Top 1000* hits, in rank order from January, 1955 through February, 1993, based on *Billboard's* pop charts.

A ranking of the Top 40 hits, year by year.

Color photos of the Top 100 Albums, from January, 1955 through March, 1993, in rank order.

An alphabetical listing, by artist name, of the *Top 1000* hits.

An alphabetical listing, by song title of the *Top 1000* hits.

Displayed throughout this book are intriguing reproductions of the original full-page ads and reviews which appeared in *Billboard* magazine during the Seventies. The previous editions of *Top 1000 Singles* featured ads and reviews from the Fifties and Sixties.

3

AUTHOR'S NOTE

Nineteen hundred and ninety-two marked the debut of two record-setting singles that shook the annals of rock and roll history. Popular culture media worldwide reported the shocking news: the King of Rock and Roll no longer had the #1 single of the rock era! And, an overthrow of the rock era's most popular single happened not once, but twice! Both in the same year!

Since 1956, Elvis Presley securely occupied the most coveted ranking of pop singles history. For 36 years, no record spent more time at the top of *Billboard's* pop singles charts than "Don't Be Cruel"/"Hound Dog." This powerhouse two-sided single held down the #1 spot on *Billboard's* Best Sellers chart for 11 consecutive weeks and topped *Billboard's* Juke Box charts for the same amount of time.

The first successful challenger to Elvis' unimpeded reign began its stay at #1 on August 15, 1992. Thirteen weeks later, "End Of The Road" by Boyz II Men had dethroned "Don't Be Cruel"/"Hound Dog." This first #1 hit for the young vocal group went on to be the biggest hit of the rock era, for a time.

Another changing of the guard began soon after, on November 28, 1992. Pop diva Whitney Houston scored her tenth #1 single with "I Will Always Love You." The blockbuster ballad easily surpassed "Don't Be Cruel"/"Hound Dog" and spent one more week at the top of the pop charts than "End Of The Road."

"I Will Always Love You" currently maintains the record for the longest stay at the top of *Billboard's Hot 100,* 14 weeks. However, as evidenced in 1992, no such record is unsurpassable.

The ultimate goal of every record that hits *Billboard's Hot 100* is to climb all the way to the top. The records that do make it to #1 are few. While a single is at the chart's summit, it is clearly the most popular song in America. Although that single is heads above its contemporaries, it is in another competition with all of the #1 hits before it. It is in an endurance match to sustain its run at #1, all the while battling the challengers to its position. The longer the run, the higher its ranking in rock and roll history.

This fierce competition makes this Top 1000 ranking dramatic, dynamic and unpredictable. No doubt future #1 hits will challenge Whitney's crowning achievement. Will 14 weeks remain the longest run at #1? If not, when and who will score the next record-breaking single? That is the thrill of watching the #1s rankings shuffle—trying to predict the next major upset in this ongoing competition.

Keep your eyes on the charts!

JOEL WHITBURN

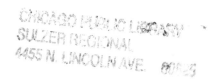

THE RANKING SYSTEM

The ranking methodology used to cover these 38+ years of hits logical and simple one based on the principle that the highest positio which a record peaks is the single most important factor during its chart Climbing its way to the upper echelons of the chart is a battle each hit rec wages in the never-ending race for chart superiority. And when its char is over, the position at which it peaked is the key statistic reflected upor music professionals and is also the primary statistic used in the rankings this book. Simply put, all #1 records will be ranked above records peaked at #2.

This *Top 1000* ranking includes every record that peaked at position plus over 45% of the records that peaked at #2, beginning with the Jul 1955 chart and ending with the February 27, 1993 *Hot 100* chart. February 17, 1993 chart marked the final week of Whitney Houston's week reign at the #1 position with "I Will Always Love You."

Following is the chronology used in ranking the *Top 1000* hits:

1) Peak position

    a) All records peaking at #1 are listed first, followed by records peaking at #2.

    b) Ties among each highest position grouping are broken in the following order:

2) Total weeks record held its peak position

3) Total weeks charted in the Top 10

4) Total weeks charted in the Top 40

5) Total weeks charted

If there are still ties, a computerized inverse point system is used calculate a point total for each record based on its weekly chart positic For each week a record appears on the charts it is given points based or chart position for that week (#1=100 points, #2=99 points, etc.). Th points are added together to create a raw point total for each record, wl is used to break any remaining ties.

The *BILLBOARD* charts were used exclusively in compiling this data. the years 1955-1958, the following *Billboard* pop charts were researct with each record's highest position taken from whichever it attaine higher ranking: *Top 100, Best Sellers, Most Played by Jockeys* and *M Played in Juke Boxes*. From August of 1958 to the present, the sole encompassing pop chart used was *Billboard's Hot 100 Singles*.

THE RANKING

This section lists, in rank order, the *Top 1000* hits from January, 1955 through February, 1993. The **peak position** and the **total weeks at the peak position** are highlighted above each group of corresponding titles.

Columnar headings show the following data:

YR: Year record reached its peak position

WEEKS: **10** - Total weeks charted in the Top 10
40 - Total weeks charted in the Top 40
CH - Total weeks charted

RANK: *Top 1000* ranking (highlighted in dark type)

GOLD: ● - RIAA certified gold record (million seller)*
▲ - RIAA certified platinum record (two million seller)*

SYM (type of recording):
[I] Instrumental
[N] Novelty
[C] Comedy
[F] Foreign language
[X] Christmas
[S] Spoken word

TIME: Playing time of each record

A small check-off circle is provided next to each title to aid in keeping track of the *Top 1000* records in your collection.

The Recording Industry Association of America (RIAA) began certifying gold records in 1958 and platinum records in 1976. Prior to these dates, there are most certainly some hits that would have qualified for these certifications. Also, some record labels have never requested RIAA certifications for their hits. As of January 1, 1989, RIAA lowered the certification for gold singles to sales of 500,000 units and platinum to one million units.

YR	CH	40	10	RANK	GOLD	PEAK POSITION	SYM	TIME	ARTIST
						Pos 1 14 Wks			
92	26	24	16	1	O	▲ I Will Always Love You		4:32	Whitney Houston
						Pos 1 13 Wks			
92	32	28	19	2	O	▲ End of the Road		5:50	Boyz II Men
						Pos 1 11 Wks			
56	28	24	21	3	O	Don't Be Cruel/		2:03	
						Hound Dog		2:15	Elvis Presley
						Pos 1 10 Wks			
56	26	22	17	4	O	Singing The Blues		2:23	Guy Mitchell
81	26	21	15	5	O	▲ Physical		3:43	Olivia Newton-John
77	25	21	14	6	O	▲ You Light Up My Life		3:35	Debby Boone
						Pos 1 9 Wks			
59	26	22	16	7	O	Mack The Knife		3:04	Bobby Darin
57	30	22	15	8	O	All Shook Up		1:58	Elvis Presley
81	26	20	14	9	O	● Bette Davis Eyes		3:47	Kim Carnes
68	19	19	14	10	O	● Hey Jude		7:11	The Beatles
81	27	19	13	11	O	▲ Endless Love		4:26	Diana Ross & Lionel Richie
60	21	17	12	12	O	● The Theme From "A Summer Place" [I]		2:24	Percy Faith
						Pos 1 8 Wks			
55	38	25	19	13	O	Rock Around The Clock		2:08	Bill Haley & His Comets
56	37	22	16	14	O	The Wayward Wind		2:56	Gogi Grant
55	22	19	16	15	O	Sixteen Tons		2:34	Tennessee Ernie Ford
56	27	22	15	16	O	Heartbreak Hotel		2:06	Elvis Presley
83	22	20	13	17	O	● Every Breath You Take		4:13	The Police
92	21	18	13	18	O	▲ Jump		3:12	Kris Kross
78	20	18	13	19	O	▲ Night Fever		3:32	Bee Gees
76	23	17	11	20	O	● Tonight's The Night (Gonna Be Alright)		3:55	Rod Stewart
						Pos 1 7 Wks			
57	34	24	17	21	O	Love Letters In The Sand		2:12	Pat Boone
57	27	19	15	22	O	Jailhouse Rock		2:10	Elvis Presley
57	25	18	14	23	O	(Let Me Be Your) Teddy Bear		1:43	Elvis Presley
78	25	19	12	24	O	▲ Shadow Dancing		4:34	Andy Gibb
58	21	18	12	25	O	At The Hop		2:31	Danny & The Juniors
61	23	17	12	26	O	Tossin' And Turnin'		2:40	Bobby Lewis
82	20	16	12	27	O	▲ I Love Rock 'N Roll		2:45	Joan Jett & The Blackhearts
82	19	15	12	28	O	● Ebony And Ivory		3:41	Paul McCartney/Stevie Wonder
64	15	14	12	29	O	● I Want To Hold Your Hand		2:24	The Beatles
66	15	13	12	30	O	● I'm A Believer		2:41	The Monkees
83	24	17	11	31	O	▲ Billie Jean		4:50	Michael Jackson
68	15	15	11	32	O	I Heard It Through The Grapevine		2:59	Marvin Gaye
91	22	17	10	33	O	▲ (Everything I Do) I Do It For You		4:03	Bryan Adams
91	20	15	10	34	O	▲ Black Or White		3:19	Michael Jackson
						Pos 1 6 Wks			
55	21	21	17	35	O	Love Is A Many-Splendored Thing		2:56	Four Aces featuring Al Alberts
56	25	20	16	36	O	Rock And Roll Waltz		2:53	Kay Starr
56	24	20	16	37	O	The Poor People Of Paris [I]		2:24	Les Baxter

YR	CH	40	10	RANK	G O L D	PEAK POSITION	PEAK WEEKS	S Y M	TIME	ARTIST

Pos 1 6 Wks Cont'd

YR	CH	40	10	RANK	GOLD	TITLE	SYM	TIME	ARTIST
55	19	19	16	38	O	The Yellow Rose Of Texas		3:00	Mitch Miller
78	25	19	15	39	O ▲	Le Freak		3:30	Chic
56	24	19	15	40	O	Memories Are Made Of This		2:15	Dean Martin
82	25	18	15	41	O ▲	Eye Of The Tiger		3:45	Survivor
83	25	20	14	42	O ●	Flashdance...What A Feeling		3:55	Irene Cara
57	26	19	14	43	O	April Love		2:39	Pat Boone
80	25	19	13	44	O ●	Lady		3:51	Kenny Rogers
83	22	18	13	45	O ▲	Say Say Say		3:55	Paul McCartney & Michael Jackson
59	21	18	13	46	O ●	The Battle Of New Orleans		2:33	Johnny Horton
57	21	17	13	47	O	Young Love		2:24	Tab Hunter
82	25	20	12	48	O ●	Centerfold		3:35	The J. Geils Band
80	25	19	12	49	O ●	Call Me		3:30	Blondie
58	22	19	12	50	O	It's All In The Game [R]		2:25	Tommy Edwards
79	22	16	12	51	O ●	My Sharona		3:58	The Knack
69	17	16	11	52	O ▲	Aquarius/Let The Sunshine In		4:45	The 5th Dimension
72	18	15	11	53	O ●	The First Time Ever I Saw Your Face		4:15	Roberta Flack
72	18	15	11	54	O ●	Alone Again (Naturally)		3:40	Gilbert O'Sullivan
71	17	15	11	55	O ●	Joy To The World		3:17	Three Dog Night
60	16	14	11	56	O ●	Are You Lonesome To-night?		3:07	Elvis Presley
58	14	14	10	57	O	The Purple People Eater [N]		2:11	Sheb Wooley
70	14	13	10	58	O ●	Bridge Over Troubled Water		4:55	Simon & Garfunkel
84	19	14	9	59	O ●	Like A Virgin		3:35	Madonna
69	13	12	9	60	O ●	In The Year 2525 (Exordium & Terminus)		3:15	Zager & Evans

Pos 1 5 Wks

YR	CH	40	10	RANK	GOLD	TITLE	SYM	TIME	ARTIST
57	31	23	16	61	O	Tammy		3:00	Debbie Reynolds
92	28	24	15	62	O ▲	Baby Got Back		4:24	Sir Mix-A-Lot
56	23	19	15	63	O	Love Me Tender		2:42	Elvis Presley
56	23	20	14	64	O	My Prayer		2:45	The Platters
80	22	19	14	65	O ●	(Just Like) Starting Over		3:54	John Lennon
92	27	23	13	66	O ●	Save The Best For Last		3:39	Vanessa Williams
77	23	17	12	67	O ●	Best Of My Love		3:40	Emotions
58	19	16	12	68	O ●	All I Have To Do Is Dream		2:17	The Everly Brothers
84	21	16	11	69	O ▲	When Doves Cry		3:49	Prince
60	20	16	11	70	O ●	It's Now Or Never		3:12	Elvis Presley
58	19	16	11	71	O	Tequila [I]		2:09	The Champs
70	16	16	11	72	O	I'll Be There		3:35	The Jackson 5
76	19	15	11	73	O ●	Silly Love Songs		5:54	Wings
71	17	15	11	74	O ●	Maggie May		5:15	Rod Stewart
62	18	14	11	75	O ●	I Can't Stop Loving You		2:37	Ray Charles
58	20	16	10	76	O ●	Don't		2:48	Elvis Presley
84	21	15	10	77	O ●	Jump		4:04	Van Halen
79	20	15	10	78	O ▲	Bad Girls		3:55	Donna Summer
68	18	15	10	79	O ●	Love Is Blue [I]		2:31	Paul Mauriat
71	17	15	10	80	O ●	It's Too Late		3:51	Carole King
59	17	14	10	81	O	Venus		2:21	Frankie Avalon
62	16	14	10	82	O	Big Girls Don't Cry		2:25	The 4 Seasons
58	16	13	10	83	O	Nel Blu Dipinto Di Blu (Volare) [F]		3:29	Domenico Modugno
61	16	13	10	84	O ●	Big Bad John [S]		2:57	Jimmy Dean
63	15	13	10	85	O ●	Sugar Shack		2:01	Jimmy Gilmer & The Fireballs
68	15	13	10	86	O ●	Honey		3:58	Bobby Goldsboro
91	19	15	9	87	O ●	Rush, Rush		4:14	Paula Abdul
67	17	15	9	88	O ●	To Sir With Love		2:44	Lulu

YR	WEEKS			RANK	GOLD	PEAK POSITION	PEAK WEEKS	SYM	TIME	ARTIST
	CH	40	10							

Pos **1** 5 Wks Cont'd

YR	CH	40	10	RANK	GOLD	SONG	SYM	TIME	ARTIST
60	17	13	9	89	O	Cathy's Clown		2:22	The Everly Brothers
73	16	13	9	90	O ●	Killing Me Softly With His Song		4:46	Roberta Flack
68	14	13	9	91	O ●	People Got To Be Free		2:57	The Rascals
71	15	12	9	92	O ●	One Bad Apple		2:45	The Osmonds
69	12	12	9	93	O ●	Get Back		3:08	The Beatles with Billy Preston
66	13	11	9	94	O ●	The Ballad Of The Green Berets		2:27	SSgt Barry Sadler
62	14	12	7	95	O	Sherry		2:07	The 4 Seasons
64	10	9	6	96	O ●	Can't Buy Me Love		2:12	The Beatles

Pos **1** 4 Wks

YR	CH	40	10	RANK	GOLD	SONG	SYM	TIME	ARTIST
55	26	26	18	97	O	Autumn Leaves	[I]	2:52	Roger Williams
56	29	24	17	98	O	Lisbon Antigua	[I]	2:33	Nelson Riddle
77	31	23	16	99	O ●	I Just Want To Be Your Everything		3:32	Andy Gibb
56	23	19	14	100	O	I Almost Lost My Mind		2:27	Pat Boone

♪   ♪   ♪   ♪   ♪   ♪

YR	CH	40	10	RANK	GOLD	SONG	SYM	TIME	ARTIST
80	29	17	14	101	O ●	Upside Down		3:37	Diana Ross
57	28	23	13	102	O	Honeycomb		2:14	Jimmie Rodgers
78	27	22	13	103	O ▲	Stayin' Alive		3:29	Bee Gees
70	22	19	13	104	O ●	Raindrops Keep Fallin' On My Head		3:02	B.J. Thomas
83	24	17	13	105	O ●	All Night Long (All Night)		4:16	Lionel Richie
82	23	17	13	106	O ●	Maneater		4:30	Daryl Hall & John Oates
57	26	20	12	107	O	Wake Up Little Susie		1:57	The Everly Brothers
80	25	19	12	108	O ●	Another Brick In The Wall (Part II)		3:10	Pink Floyd
58	23	19	12	109	O	Sugartime		2:29	The McGuire Sisters
69	22	18	12	110	O ●	Sugar, Sugar		2:48	The Archies
79	21	18	12	111	O ▲	Da Ya Think I'm Sexy?		5:21	Rod Stewart
78	23	17	12	112	O ●	Kiss You All Over		3:30	Exile
80	22	17	12	113	O ●	Crazy Little Thing Called Love		2:44	Queen
83	29	18	11	114	O ●	Total Eclipse Of The Heart		4:29	Bonnie Tyler
73	23	17	11	115	O ●	Tie A Yellow Ribbon Round The Ole Oak Tree		3:19	Dawn Featuring Tony Orlando
72	19	17	11	116	O ●	American Pie - Parts I & II		8:36	Don McLean
70	17	15	11	117	O ●	(They Long To Be) Close To You		3:40	Carpenters
68	16	14	11	118	O ●	(Sittin' On) The Dock Of The Bay		2:38	Otis Redding
69	15	14	11	119	O ●	Honky Tonk Women		3:03	The Rolling Stones
83	25	19	10	120	O ●	Down Under		3:41	Men At Work
86	23	17	10	121	O ●	That's What Friends Are For		3:58	Dionne & Friends
82	22	17	10	122	O ●	Jack & Diane		4:16	John Cougar
90	23	16	10	123	O ●	Because I Love You (The Postman Song)		4:15	Stevie B
79	23	15	10	124	O ▲	Reunited		3:58	Peaches & Herb
90	21	15	10	125	O ▲	Nothing Compares 2 U		5:09	Sinead O'Connor
59	21	15	10	126	O	Stagger Lee		2:20	Lloyd Price
89	18	14	10	127	O ●	Another Day In Paradise		4:48	Phil Collins
59	17	14	10	128	O	The Three Bells		2:47	The Browns
59	15	14	10	129	O	Lonely Boy		2:33	Paul Anka
71	15	14	10	130	O ●	How Can You Mend A Broken Heart		3:52	The Bee Gees
60	16	13	10	131	O	Stuck On You		2:17	Elvis Presley
62	15	13	10	132	O ●	Roses Are Red (My Love)		2:37	Bobby Vinton
70	14	13	10	133	O ●	My Sweet Lord		4:39	George Harrison
67	16	12	10	134	O ●	Daydream Believer		2:57	The Monkees
80	24	19	9	135	O ▲	Rock With You		3:20	Michael Jackson
80	23	16	9	136	O ●	Magic		4:25	Olivia Newton-John
85	20	16	9	137	O ●	Say You, Say Me		3:59	Lionel Richie
80	23	15	9	138	O ▲	Funkytown		3:57	Lipps, Inc.

YR	WEEKS			RANK	G O L D	PEAK POSITION	PEAK WEEKS	S Y M	TIME	ARTIST
	CH	40	10							

Pos 1 4 Wks Cont'd

YR	CH	40	10	RANK	GOLD	TITLE		SYM	TIME	ARTIST
87	20	15	9	139	O ●	Faith			3:14	George Michael
73	18	15	9	140	O ●	My Love			4:07	Paul McCartney & Wings
69	19	14	9	141	O ●	Everyday People			2:18	Sly & The Family Stone
72	19	14	9	142	O ●	Without You			3:16	Nilsson
58	19	14	9	143	O ●	He's Got The Whole World (In His Hands)			2:20	Laurie London
69	15	13	9	144	O ●	Dizzy			2:55	Tommy Roe
67	14	13	9	145	O ●	Windy			2:49	The Association
67	20	12	9	146	O ●	Ode To Billie Joe			4:13	Bobbie Gentry
61	17	12	9	147	O	Runaway			2:20	Del Shannon
63	15	12	9	148	O	He's So Fine			1:53	The Chiffons
65	14	12	9	149	O ●	(I Can't Get No) Satisfaction			3:45	The Rolling Stones
63	13	12	9	150	O	Dominique	[F]		2:53	The Singing Nun
64	13	12	9	151	O	There! I've Said It Again			2:20	Bobby Vinton
67	13	11	9	152	O ●	Somethin' Stupid			2:35	Nancy Sinatra & Frank Sinatra
67	13	11	9	153	O ●	Groovin'			2:25	The Young Rascals
86	23	15	8	154	O ●	Walk Like An Egyptian			3:21	Bangles
76	20	15	8	155	O ●	Don't Go Breaking My Heart			4:23	Elton John & Kiki Dee
72	20	14	8	156	O ●	I Can See Clearly Now			2:48	Johnny Nash
89	20	13	8	157	O ▲	Miss You Much			3:55	Janet Jackson
76	19	13	8	158	O ▲	Disco Lady			4:20	Johnnie Taylor
67	16	13	8	159	O ●	The Letter			1:58	The Box Tops
85	18	12	8	160	O ▲	We Are The World			6:22	USA for Africa
59	16	12	8	161	O	Come Softly To Me			2:25	Fleetwoods
68	14	12	8	162	O ●	This Guy's In Love With You			3:55	Herb Alpert
64	13	12	8	163	O ●	Baby Love			2:34	The Supremes
90	22	17	7	164	O ●	Vision Of Love			3:22	Mariah Carey
88	18	14	7	165	O	Roll With It			4:30	Steve Winwood
87	21	13	7	166	O	Livin' On A Prayer			4:12	Bon Jovi
75	23	16	6	167	O ●	Love Will Keep Us Together			3:15	The Captain & Tennille
58	28	13	6	168	O	The Chipmunk Song	[X-N]		2:17	The Chipmunks/David Seville
65	11	9	6	169	O ●	Yesterday			2:04	The Beatles

Pos 1 3 Wks

YR	CH	40	10	RANK	GOLD	TITLE		SYM	TIME	ARTIST
60	39	33	25	170	O	The Twist			2:32	Chubby Checker
56	26	22	18	171	O	The Green Door			2:11	Jim Lowe
77	33	26	17	172	O ●	How Deep Is Your Love			3:30	Bee Gees
56	27	22	15	173	O	Moonglow and Theme From "Picnic"	[I]		2:47	Morris Stoloff
80	31	21	15	174	O ▲	Another One Bites The Dust			3:32	Queen
79	21	17	14	175	O ▲	Hot Stuff			3:47	Donna Summer
77	25	18	13	176	O ●	Love Theme From "A Star Is Born" (Evergreen)			3:03	Barbra Streisand
79	27	17	13	177	O ▲	I Will Survive			3:15	Gloria Gaynor
57	26	17	13	178	O	You Send Me			2:41	Sam Cooke
82	28	21	12	179	O ●	Don't You Want Me			3:56	The Human League
58	19	18	12	180	O	Witch Doctor	[N]		2:15	David Seville
81	24	17	12	181	O ●	Arthur's Theme (Best That You Can Do)			3:53	Christopher Cross
78	23	17	12	182	O ▲	Boogie Oogie Oogie			3:45	A Taste Of Honey
92	21	17	12	183	O ▲	I'm Too Sexy	[N]		2:50	Right Said Fred
80	24	19	11	184	O ●	Woman In Love			3:48	Barbra Streisand
60	23	18	11	185	O	I'm Sorry			2:40	Brenda Lee
58	23	18	11	186	O	To Know Him, Is To Love Him			2:18	The Teddy Bears
84	23	16	11	187	O ▲	Footloose			3:46	Kenny Loggins
80	21	16	11	188	O ●	Coming Up (Live at Glasgow)			3:54	Paul McCartney & Wings
70	19	16	11	189	O ●	I Think I Love You			2:28	The Partridge Family

YR	CH	40	10	RANK	G O L D	PEAK POSITION		S Y M	TIME	ARTIST

Pos **1** 3 Wks Cont'd

YR	CH	40	10	RANK	GOLD	TITLE	SYM	TIME	ARTIST
71	18	16	11	190	O ●	Knock Three Times		2:56	Dawn
62	18	14	11	191	O	Peppermint Twist - Part I		2:00	Joey Dee & the Starliters
73	17	14	11	192	O ●	You're So Vain		4:25	Carly Simon
84	28	18	10	193	O ●	What's Love Got To Do With It		3:49	Tina Turner
83	25	18	10	194	O ▲	Beat It		4:11	Michael Jackson
76	25	18	10	195	O ▲	Play That Funky Music		3:12	Wild Cherry
78	32	16	10	196	O ●	Baby Come Back		3:28	Player
84	24	16	10	197	O ●	Against All Odds (Take A Look At Me Now)		3:24	Phil Collins
79	21	16	10	198	O ●	Escape (The Pina Colada Song)		3:50	Rupert Holmes
59	19	16	10	199	O	Smoke Gets In Your Eyes		2:39	The Platters
84	26	15	10	200	O ●	I Just Called To Say I Love You		4:16	Stevie Wonder

♪　♪　♪　♪　♪　♪

YR	CH	40	10	RANK	GOLD	TITLE	SYM	TIME	ARTIST
61	17	15	10	201	O	Wonderland By Night	[I]	3:12	Bert Kaempfert
60	27	14	10	202	O	Running Bear		2:33	Johnny Preston
84	21	14	10	203	O ●	Ghostbusters		3:46	Ray Parker Jr.
57	20	14	10	204	O	Butterfly		2:17	Andy Williams
71	18	14	10	205	O ●	Brand New Key		2:26	Melanie
66	15	13	10	206	O ●	Winchester Cathedral		2:23	The New Vaudeville Band
72	14	12	10	207	O ●	A Horse With No Name		4:10	America
92	24	17	9	208	O ●	To Be With You		3:20	Mr. Big
74	23	17	9	209	O ●	The Way We Were		3:29	Barbra Streisand
85	21	17	9	210	O ▲	Careless Whisper		4:50	Wham! Featuring George Michael
84	22	16	9	211	O ●	Karma Chameleon		4:05	Culture Club
78	20	15	9	212	O ●	MacArthur Park		3:59	Donna Summer
67	23	14	9	213	O ●	Light My Fire		2:52	The Doors
60	18	14	9	214	O	Save The Last Dance For Me		2:34	The Drifters
73	17	14	9	215	O ●	Crocodile Rock		3:56	Elton John
57	17	14	9	216	O	Too Much		2:30	Elvis Presley
72	18	13	9	217	O ●	Baby Don't Get Hooked On Me		3:02	Mac Davis
71	15	13	9	218	O ●	Go Away Little Girl		2:30	Donny Osmond
71	14	13	9	219	O ●	Family Affair		3:04	Sly & The Family Stone
70	14	13	9	220	O	Ain't No Mountain High Enough		3:15	Diana Ross
67	15	12	9	221	O ●	Happy Together		2:50	The Turtles
63	15	12	9	222	O ●	Hey Paula		2:25	Paul & Paula
63	14	12	9	223	O	My Boyfriend's Back		2:11	The Angels
81	23	17	8	224	O ●	Kiss On My List		3:48	Daryl Hall & John Oates
90	24	16	8	225	O ▲	Vogue		4:19	Madonna
74	21	15	8	226	O ●	Seasons In The Sun		3:24	Terry Jacks
87	21	15	8	227	O	Alone		3:38	Heart
90	17	15	8	228	O ●	Escapade		4:41	Janet Jackson
84	24	14	8	229	O ▲	Wake Me Up Before You Go-Go		3:51	Wham!
88	21	14	8	230	O ●	Every Rose Has Its Thorn		4:20	Poison
85	18	14	8	231	O ●	Can't Fight This Feeling		4:54	REO Speedwagon
61	16	14	8	232	O	Pony Time		2:27	Chubby Checker
72	16	14	8	233	O ●	Me And Mrs. Jones		4:42	Billy Paul
64	15	14	8	234	O ●	Oh, Pretty Woman		2:55	Roy Orbison
70	15	14	8	235	O ●	American Woman		3:51	The Guess Who
69	15	14	8	236	O ▲	Wedding Bell Blues		2:42	The 5th Dimension
85	22	13	8	237	O	Money For Nothing		4:38	Dire Straits
87	18	13	8	238	O	With Or Without You		4:56	U2
77	17	13	8	239	O	Sir Duke		3:53	Stevie Wonder
62	16	13	8	240	O	Telstar	[I]	3:14	The Tornadoes
70	15	13	8	241	O	War		3:12	Edwin Starr

YR	CH	40	10	RANK	GOLD	PEAK POSITION	SYM	TIME	ARTIST

Pos **1** 3 Wks Cont'd

YR	CH	40	10	RANK	GOLD	PEAK POSITION	SYM	TIME	ARTIST
61	15	13	8	242	O ●	The Lion Sleeps Tonight		2:35	The Tokens
62	14	13	8	243	O	Soldier Boy		2:40	The Shirelles
74	17	12	8	244	O ●	The Streak	[N]	3:15	Ray Stevens
63	15	12	8	245	O	Blue Velvet		2:46	Bobby Vinton
62	15	12	8	246	O	Hey! Baby		2:23	Bruce Channel
63	14	12	8	247	O	Sukiyaki	[F]	3:05	Kyu Sakamoto
62	15	11	8	248	O	Duke Of Earl		2:22	Gene Chandler
65	14	11	8	249	O	Turn! Turn! Turn! (To Everything There Is A Season)		3:34	The Byrds
61	14	11	8	250	O	Blue Moon		2:15	The Marcels
63	14	11	8	251	O	I Will Follow Him		2:25	Little Peggy March
66	13	11	8	252	O ●	(You're My) Soul And Inspiration		3:00	The Righteous Brothers
66	12	10	8	253	O ●	Monday, Monday		3:09	The Mama's & The Papa's
67	11	10	8	254	O ●	Hello Goodbye		3:24	The Beatles
64	11	10	8	255	O	The House Of The Rising Sun		2:58	The Animals
91	20	20	7	256	O ●	Emotions		4:09	Mariah Carey
90	26	18	7	257	O ●	Love Takes Time		3:40	Mariah Carey
89	25	16	7	258	O ▲	Straight Up		4:11	Paula Abdul
72	21	16	7	259	O ●	The Candy Man		3:10	Sammy Davis, Jr.
82	23	15	7	260	O ▲	Up Where We Belong		4:00	Joe Cocker & Jennifer Warnes
86	23	15	7	261	O ●	On My Own		4:30	Patti LaBelle & Michael McDonald
90	23	14	7	262	O ●	Opposites Attract		3:45	Paula Abdul with The Wild Pair
87	21	14	7	263	O	La Bamba	[F]	2:54	Los Lobos
72	19	14	7	264	O ●	Lean On Me		3:45	Bill Withers
86	18	14	7	265	O	Greatest Love Of All		4:30	Whitney Houston
88	18	14	7	266	O ●	One More Try		5:50	George Michael
89	21	13	7	267	O ▲	Right Here Waiting		4:21	Richard Marx
85	19	13	7	268	O ●	Shout		3:59	Tears For Fears
86	19	13	7	269	O	Stuck With You		4:20	Huey Lewis & the News
75	17	13	7	270	O ●	Fly, Robin, Fly	[I]	3:05	Silver Convention
86	17	13	7	271	O	Rock Me Amadeus		3:10	Falco
89	19	12	7	272	O ●	Lost In Your Eyes		3:34	Debbie Gibson
89	16	12	7	273	O ▲	Like A Prayer		5:19	Madonna
75	15	12	7	274	O ●	Island Girl		3:46	Elton John
63	15	12	7	275	O	Fingertips - Pt 2		2:49	Little Stevie Wonder
68	13	12	7	276	O ●	Mrs. Robinson		4:00	Simon & Garfunkel
63	13	12	7	277	O	Walk Like A Man		2:11	The 4 Seasons
61	15	11	7	278	O	Take Good Care Of My Baby		2:27	Bobby Vee
90	15	11	7	279	O ▲	Step By Step		4:18	New Kids On The Block
64	13	11	7	280	O	Chapel Of Love		2:45	The Dixie Cups
66	12	11	7	281	O ●	We Can Work It Out		2:10	The Beatles
65	11	11	7	282	O ●	Mrs. Brown You've Got A Lovely Daughter		2:46	Herman's Hermits
64	11	11	7	283	O ●	I Feel Fine		2:20	The Beatles
65	14	10	7	284	O ●	I Got You Babe		3:09	Sonny & Cher
66	11	10	7	285	O ●	Summer In The City		2:39	The Lovin' Spoonful
90	23	16	6	286	O	How Am I Supposed To Live Without You		4:14	Michael Bolton
76	27	15	6	287	O ●	December, 1963 (Oh, What a Night)		3:21	The Four Seasons
76	17	13	6	288	O ●	50 Ways To Leave Your Lover		3:29	Paul Simon
66	14	12	6	289	O ●	Cherish		3:00	The Association
65	13	12	6	290	O ●	Help!		2:16	The Beatles
74	15	11	6	291	O ●	(You're) Having My Baby		2:32	Paul Anka
75	14	10	6	292	O ●	He Don't Love You (Like I Love You)		3:36	Tony Orlando & Dawn
75	14	12	5	293	O ●	Bad Blood		3:06	Neil Sedaka

13

LIFT OFF!

On the morning of April 16, 1972, Apollo 16 was launched into orbit on a journey to the moon. A few mornings earlier Uni Records launched a new Elton John single into a world-wide orbit. WHAT A TRIP! Both launchings bound to set new records.

ELTON JOHN
★
ROCKET MAN

Produced by Gus Dudgeon   Uni 55328

MCA Records, Inc.

her new single
Joan Baez
SINGS
"the night they drove old dixie down" VRS-35138

WRITTEN BY J. ROBBIE ROBERTSON
RECORDED IN NASHVILLE   PRODUCED BY NORBERT PUTNAM/ JACK LOTHROP CO-PRODUCER

Available in all tape configurations from Ampex

YR	WEEKS			RANK	GOLD	PEAK POSITION	PEAK WEEKS	SYM	TIME	ARTIST
	CH	40	10							

Pos 1 2 Wks

YR	CH	40	10	RANK	GOLD	TITLE	SYM	TIME	ARTIST
55	21	21	18	294	O	Learnin' The Blues		2:59	Frank Sinatra
55	20	20	15	295	O	Ain't That A Shame		2:22	Pat Boone
57	29	19	14	296	O	Round And Round		2:30	Perry Como
82	25	19	14	297	O ●	Abracadabra		3:34	The Steve Miller Band
56	24	19	14	298	O	The Great Pretender		2:38	The Platters
73	19	17	13	299	O	Let's Get It On		3:58	Marvin Gaye
81	32	22	12	300	O ●	Jessie's Girl		3:14	Rick Springfield

♪   ♪   ♪   ♪   ♪   ♪

YR	CH	40	10	RANK	GOLD	TITLE	SYM	TIME	ARTIST
83	25	18	12	301	O ▲	Islands In The Stream		4:08	Kenny Rogers & Dolly Parton
82	24	18	12	302	O ●	Hard To Say I'm Sorry		3:42	Chicago
78	29	22	11	303	O ●	(Love Is) Thicker Than Water		3:18	Andy Gibb
80	21	19	11	304	O ●	It's Still Rock And Roll To Me		2:55	Billy Joel
78	20	16	11	305	O	Three Times A Lady		3:35	Commodores
79	21	15	11	306	O	Ring My Bell		3:30	Anita Ward
69	17	15	11	307	O	I Can't Get Next To You		2:53	The Temptations
68	16	15	11	308	O	Love Child		2:59	Diana Ross & The Supremes
69	16	15	11	309	O	Crimson And Clover		3:23	Tommy James & The Shondells
58	15	15	11	310	O	Poor Little Fool		2:29	Ricky Nelson
79	19	14	11	311	O ●	Babe		4:26	Styx
64	15	14	11	312	O	She Loves You		2:18	The Beatles
70	14	13	11	313	O ●	Let It Be		3:50	The Beatles
84	24	17	10	314	O ●	Hello		4:07	Lionel Richie
84	23	17	10	315	O	Owner Of A Lonely Heart		3:50	Yes
58	21	17	10	316	O	It's Only Make Believe		2:10	Conway Twitty
77	22	16	10	317	O ●	Torn Between Two Lovers		3:40	Mary MacGregor
59	20	16	10	318	O	Heartaches By The Number		2:39	Guy Mitchell
92	20	16	10	319	O ●	How Do You Talk To An Angel		3:40	The Heights
73	19	16	10	320	O	Keep On Truckin' (Part 1)		3:21	Eddie Kendricks
78	17	15	10	321	O ●	You Don't Bring Me Flowers		3:14	Barbra Streisand & Neil Diamond
60	18	14	10	322	O	Teen Angel		2:38	Mark Dinning
60	17	14	10	323	O	My Heart Has A Mind Of Its Own		2:25	Connie Francis
70	16	14	10	324	O	The Tears Of A Clown		2:56	Smokey Robinson & The Miracles
82	18	13	10	325	O ●	Truly		3:19	Lionel Richie
65	14	13	10	326	O	I Can't Help Myself		2:43	Four Tops
83	32	18	9	327	O ●	Baby, Come To Me		3:30	Patti Austin with James Ingram
81	28	18	9	328	O ●	I Love A Rainy Night		3:08	Eddie Rabbitt
81	26	18	9	329	O ●	9 To 5		2:42	Dolly Parton
75	23	18	9	330	O ●	Rhinestone Cowboy		3:08	Glen Campbell
76	26	17	9	331	O ▲	Kiss And Say Goodbye		3:29	Manhattans
91	25	17	9	332	O ▲	Gonna Make You Sweat (Everybody Dance Now)		4:03	C & C Music Factory
90	25	17	9	333	O ●	It Must Have Been Love		3:43	Roxette
81	23	17	9	334	O ●	Private Eyes		3:29	Daryl Hall & John Oates
75	21	17	9	335	O ●	Philadelphia Freedom		5:38	The Elton John Band
76	21	17	9	336	O ●	If You Leave Me Now		3:53	Chicago
79	21	17	9	337	O ▲	Too Much Heaven		4:54	Bee Gees
84	23	16	9	338	O ●	Out Of Touch		3:55	Daryl Hall John Oates
83	22	16	9	339	O	Maniac		4:13	Michael Sembello
60	22	16	9	340	O	El Paso		4:40	Marty Robbins
79	25	15	9	341	O ●	Rise	[I]	3:47	Herb Alpert
85	22	15	9	342	O	Broken Wings		4:29	Mr. Mister
84	20	14	9	343	O ●	Time After Time		3:59	Cyndi Lauper
84	19	14	9	344	O ▲	Let's Hear It For The Boy		4:20	Deniece Williams
84	19	14	9	345	O ●	Let's Go Crazy		3:46	Prince & the Revolution

YR	CH	40	10	RANK	GOLD	PEAK POSITION	SYM	TIME	ARTIST
						Pos **1 2** Wks Cont'd			
87	18	14	9	346	O ▲	I Wanna Dance With Somebody (Who Loves Me)		4:36	Whitney Houston
71	16	14	9	347	O ●	Gypsys, Tramps & Thieves		2:36	Cher
79	20	13	9	348	O ▲	Tragedy		5:00	Bee Gees
76	18	13	9	349	O	Love Hangover		3:40	Diana Ross
59	18	13	9	350	O	Sleep Walk	[I]	2:20	Santo & Johnny
61	17	13	9	351	O ●	Calcutta	[I]	2:13	Lawrence Welk
65	16	13	9	352	O	You've Lost That Lovin' Feelin'		3:05	The Righteous Brothers
75	16	13	9	353	O	That's The Way (I Like It)		3:06	KC & The Sunshine Band
64	15	13	9	354	O ●	I Get Around		2:12	The Beach Boys
71	15	13	9	355	O	Just My Imagination (Running Away With Me)		3:39	The Temptations
65	15	13	9	356	O ●	Downtown		2:58	Petula Clark
62	15	13	9	357	O	Johnny Angel		2:16	Shelley Fabares
70	15	13	9	358	O ●	Mama Told Me (Not To Come)		2:58	Three Dog Night
68	15	13	9	359	O ●	Tighten Up		2:38	Archie Bell & The Drells
79	15	13	9	360	O ●	No More Tears (Enough Is Enough)		4:39	Barbra Streisand/Donna Summer
64	14	13	9	361	O	Come See About Me		2:39	The Supremes
64	14	13	9	362	O	Where Did Our Love Go		2:32	The Supremes
63	17	12	9	363	O	Go Away Little Girl		2:07	Steve Lawrence
61	14	12	9	364	O	Runaround Sue		2:40	Dion
70	13	12	9	365	O	ABC		2:38	The Jackson 5
70	13	12	9	366	O	The Love You Save		2:42	The Jackson 5
71	13	12	9	367	O	Theme From Shaft		3:15	Isaac Hayes
64	13	12	9	368	O	Do Wah Diddy Diddy		2:19	Manfred Mann
61	17	11	9	369	O	Michael		2:45	The Highwaymen
65	12	11	9	370	O ●	This Diamond Ring		2:05	Gary Lewis & The Playboys
68	12	11	9	371	O ●	Hello, I Love You		2:13	The Doors
62	37	24	8	372	O ●	Monster Mash	[N]	3:01	Bobby "Boris" Pickett & The Crypt-Kickers
91	25	18	8	373	O ●	The First Time		4:15	Surface
88	24	16	8	374	O ●	Look Away		3:59	Chicago
73	22	16	8	375	O ●	Bad, Bad Leroy Brown		3:02	Jim Croce
85	21	16	8	376	O ●	I Want To Know What Love Is		4:58	Foreigner
73	20	16	8	377	O ●	Top Of The World		2:56	Carpenters
73	19	16	8	378	O ●	Midnight Train To Georgia		3:55	Gladys Knight & The Pips
60	18	16	8	379	O	Everybody's Somebody's Fool		2:40	Connie Francis
78	22	15	8	380	O ▲	Grease		3:21	Frankie Valli
87	22	15	8	381	O ●	Nothing's Gonna Stop Us Now		4:29	Starship
84	21	15	8	382	O ●	The Reflex		4:25	Duran Duran
85	19	15	8	383	O ●	The Power Of Love		3:53	Huey Lewis & The News
89	19	15	8	384	O ●	We Didn't Start The Fire		4:29	Billy Joel
73	18	15	8	385	O ●	Brother Louie		3:55	Stories
61	16	15	8	386	O ●	Travelin' Man		2:12	Ricky Nelson
85	24	14	8	387	O	Everybody Wants To Rule The World		4:10	Tears For Fears
73	22	14	8	388	O ●	Will It Go Round In Circles		3:42	Billy Preston
73	20	14	8	389	O ●	Half-Breed		2:42	Cher
92	20	14	8	390	O	I'll Be There		4:12	Mariah Carey
81	20	14	8	391	O ●	Rapture		6:33	Blondie
76	20	14	8	392	O ●	Afternoon Delight		3:12	Starland Vocal Band
91	19	14	8	393	O ●	I Don't Wanna Cry		4:49	Mariah Carey
57	17	14	8	394	O	Butterfly		2:21	Charlie Gracie
69	16	13	8	395	O ●	Na Na Hey Hey Kiss Him Goodbye		3:45	Steam
68	16	13	8	396	O ●	Judy In Disguise (With Glasses)		2:47	John Fred & His Playboy Band
91	16	13	8	397	O ▲	Justify My Love		4:50	Madonna

YR	WEEKS			RANK	G O L D	PEAK POSITION	PEAK WEEKS	S Y M	TIME	ARTIST
	CH	40	10							

Pos **1** 2 Wks Cont'd

64	15	13	8	398	O	My Guy			2:45	Mary Wells
58	15	13	8	399	O	Get A Job			2:25	The Silhouettes
78	18	12	8	400	O	With A Little Luck			5:45	Wings

♪   ♪   ♪   ♪   ♪   ♪

74	18	12	8	401	O •	Kung Fu Fighting			3:18	Carl Douglas
75	17	12	8	402	O •	Jive Talkin'			3:33	Bee Gees
59	16	12	8	403	O	Kansas City			2:21	Wilbert Harrison
71	15	12	8	404	O	Me And Bobby McGee			4:09	Janis Joplin
61	15	12	8	405	O	Quarter To Three			2:29	U.S. Bonds
69	14	12	8	406	O •	Love Theme From Romeo & Juliet	[I]		2:29	Henry Mancini
64	13	12	8	407	O •	A Hard Day's Night			2:28	The Beatles
71	12	12	8	408	O	Brown Sugar			3:50	The Rolling Stones
61	13	11	8	409	O	Hit The Road Jack			2:00	Ray Charles
66	13	11	8	410	O	You Can't Hurry Love			2:49	The Supremes
61	12	11	8	411	O	Surrender			1:51	Elvis Presley
65	12	10	8	412	O	Stop! In The Name Of Love			2:51	The Supremes
66	11	9	8	413	O	Wild Thing			2:30	The Troggs
81	30	21	7	414	O ▲	Celebration			3:42	Kool & The Gang
91	21	16	7	415	O	Baby Baby			3:44	Amy Grant
91	20	16	7	416	O •	Cream			4:08	Prince & The N.P.G.
84	26	15	7	417	O •	Caribbean Queen (No More Love On The Run)			3:32	Billy Ocean
85	24	15	7	418	O •	We Built This City			4:49	Starship
90	24	15	7	419	O •	Black Velvet			4:45	Alannah Myles
91	23	15	7	420	O •	All The Man That I Need			3:43	Whitney Houston
90	22	15	7	421	O •	Release Me			3:40	Wilson Phillips
61	19	15	7	422	O	Will You Love Me Tomorrow			2:48	The Shirelles
91	19	15	7	423	O •	Someday			3:55	Mariah Carey
88	24	14	7	424	O •	Never Gonna Give You Up			3:31	Rick Astley
88	24	14	7	425	O •	Sweet Child O' Mine			5:55	Guns N' Roses
88	23	14	7	426	O •	Anything For You			4:02	Gloria Estefan & Miami Sound Machine
85	22	14	7	427	O	St. Elmo's Fire (Man In Motion)			4:08	John Parr
91	20	14	7	428	O •	I Adore Mi Amor			4:45	Color Me Badd
73	20	14	7	429	O •	The Night The Lights Went Out In Georgia			3:36	Vicki Lawrence
88	20	14	7	430	O	Get Outta My Dreams, Get Into My Car			4:43	Billy Ocean
91	19	14	7	431	O	Coming Out Of The Dark			3:55	Gloria Estefan
90	18	14	7	432	O •	She Ain't Worth It			3:31	Glenn Medeiros/Bobby Brown
86	20	13	7	433	O	Kyrie			4:10	Mr. Mister
86	18	13	7	434	O •	Kiss			3:46	Prince & The Revolution
86	18	13	7	435	O	Papa Don't Preach			3:47	Madonna
89	18	13	7	436	O	Two Hearts			3:23	Phil Collins
87	17	13	7	437	O	I Still Haven't Found What I'm Looking For			4:36	U2
88	17	13	7	438	O	Man In The Mirror			4:55	Michael Jackson
87	17	13	7	439	O	Didn't We Almost Have It All			4:56	Whitney Houston
74	19	12	7	440	O •	Billy, Don't Be A Hero			3:25	Bo Donaldson & The Heywoods
62	18	12	7	441	O	He's A Rebel			2:25	The Crystals
87	17	12	7	442	O	I Knew You Were Waiting (For Me)			3:57	Aretha Franklin & George Michael
73	15	12	7	443	O •	Time In A Bottle			2:24	Jim Croce
66	15	12	7	444	O	Reach Out I'll Be There			2:58	Four Tops
63	15	12	7	445	O	I'm Leaving It Up To You			2:13	Dale & Grace
62	14	12	7	446	O	Breaking Up Is Hard To Do			2:20	Neil Sedaka
70	13	12	7	447	O •	Thank You (Falettinme Be Mice Elf Agin)			4:47	Sly & The Family Stone
74	17	11	7	448	O •	Annie's Song			2:58	John Denver
65	14	11	7	449	O	Help Me, Rhonda			2:45	The Beach Boys

YR	WEEKS			RANK	GOLD	PEAK POSITION	PEAK WEEKS	SYM	TIME	ARTIST
	CH	40	10							

Pos 1 2 Wks Cont'd

YR	CH	40	10	RANK	G	TITLE		TIME	ARTIST
62	13	11	7	450	O	Good Luck Charm		2:23	Elvis Presley
63	13	11	7	451	O	Surf City		2:24	Jan & Dean
63	13	11	7	452	O	It's My Party		2:19	Lesley Gore
63	13	11	7	453	O	Walk Right In		2:32	The Rooftop Singers
64	12	11	7	454	O ●	Rag Doll		2:31	The 4 Seasons
67	12	11	7	455	O ●	Respect		2:26	Aretha Franklin
59	14	10	7	456	O	A Big Hunk O' Love		2:12	Elvis Presley
63	13	10	7	457	O	Easier Said Than Done		2:08	The Essex
67	13	10	7	458	O	Kind Of A Drag		2:05	The Buckinghams
68	12	10	7	459	O ●	Grazing In The Grass	[I]	2:25	Hugh Masekela
66	11	10	7	460	O	Paint It, Black		3:19	The Rolling Stones
73	22	17	6	461	O ●	The Most Beautiful Girl		2:42	Charlie Rich
86	23	16	6	462	O	How Will I Know		4:10	Whitney Houston
87	24	15	6	463	O ●	At This Moment	[R]	4:10	Billy Vera & The Beaters
89	22	15	6	464	O ●	When I See You Smile		4:16	Bad English
81	21	15	6	465	O ●	Morning Train (Nine To Five)		3:20	Sheena Easton
88	27	14	6	466	O	The Flame		4:30	Cheap Trick
89	23	14	6	467	O ▲	Blame It On The Rain		4:06	Milli Vanilli
89	22	14	6	468	O ●	Forever Your Girl		4:12	Paula Abdul
89	22	14	6	469	O ●	Girl I'm Gonna Miss You		4:19	Milli Vanilli
86	21	14	6	470	O	Glory Of Love		4:20	Peter Cetera
75	21	14	6	471	O ●	Fame		3:30	David Bowie
74	20	14	6	472	O ●	The Loco-Motion		2:45	Grand Funk
88	20	14	6	473	O	Could've Been		3:31	Tiffany
85	20	14	6	474	O ●	Everything She Wants		5:10	Wham!
77	20	14	6	475	O ●	Rich Girl		2:23	Daryl Hall & John Oates
85	19	14	6	476	O	Heaven		4:03	Bryan Adams
74	18	14	6	477	O ●	TSOP (The Sound Of Philadelphia)	[I]	3:29	MFSB with The Three Degrees
58	16	14	6	478	O ●	Hard Headed Woman		1:52	Elvis Presley
88	26	13	6	479	O ●	Don't Worry Be Happy		3:45	Bobby McFerrin
88	25	13	6	480	O ●	Groovy Kind Of Love		3:28	Phil Collins
87	24	13	6	481	O	I Think We're Alone Now		3:47	Tiffany
89	20	13	6	482	O ●	Toy Soldiers		4:52	Martika
77	20	13	6	483	O ▲	Star Wars Theme/Cantina Band	[I]	3:28	Meco
86	19	13	6	484	O ●	When I Think Of You		3:56	Janet Jackson
87	19	13	6	485	O	(I Just) Died In Your Arms		4:38	Cutting Crew
88	18	13	6	486	O	Where Do Broken Hearts Go		4:37	Whitney Houston
85	17	13	6	487	O	A View To A Kill		3:33	Duran Duran
88	17	13	6	488	O	Father Figure		5:37	George Michael
70	15	13	6	489	O ●	Everything Is Beautiful		3:29	Ray Stevens
88	20	12	6	490	O	Bad Medicine		3:52	Bon Jovi
86	20	12	6	491	O	True Colors		3:45	Cyndi Lauper
85	18	12	6	492	O ●	One More Night		4:25	Phil Collins
86	18	12	6	493	O	Amanda		4:16	Boston
74	18	12	6	494	O ●	I Can Help		2:57	Billy Swan
87	17	12	6	495	O ●	Lean On Me		3:58	Club Nouveau
72	17	12	6	496	O ●	My Ding-A-Ling	[N]	4:18	Chuck Berry
88	16	12	6	497	O	Monkey		4:45	George Michael
73	15	11	6	498	O ●	The Morning After		2:14	Maureen McGovern
62	14	11	6	499	O ●	Sheila		2:02	Tommy Roe
63	14	11	6	500	O	If You Wanna Be Happy		2:14	Jimmy Soul
65	12	11	6	501	O	Get Off Of My Cloud		2:58	The Rolling Stones
75	14	10	6	502	O ●	Lucy In The Sky With Diamonds		5:58	Elton John

YR	CH	40	10	RANK	GOLD	PEAK POSITION	SYM	TIME	ARTIST

Pos **1** 2 Wks Cont'd

YR	CH	40	10	RANK	GOLD	TITLE	SYM	TIME	ARTIST
66	13	10	6	503	O ●	When A Man Loves A Woman		2:55	Percy Sledge
66	12	10	6	504	O	You Keep Me Hangin' On		2:45	The Supremes
66	12	10	6	505	O ●	Hanky Panky		2:59	Tommy James & The Shondells
70	10	10	6	506	O	The Long And Winding Road		3:40	The Beatles
65	10	10	6	507	O	I Hear A Symphony		2:41	The Supremes
66	13	9	6	508	O	My Love		2:50	Petula Clark
65	11	8	6	509	O	I'm Telling You Now		2:05	Freddie & The Dreamers
66	14	12	5	510	O ●	The Sounds Of Silence		3:05	Simon & Garfunkel
87	14	11	5	511	O	Bad		4:05	Michael Jackson
74	24	10	5	512	O ●	I Honestly Love You		3:36	Olivia Newton-John
74	17	10	5	513	O	Rock Your Baby		3:14	George McCrae
66	10	10	5	514	O ●	Paperback Writer		2:25	The Beatles
65	10	9	5	515	O ●	Eight Days A Week		2:43	The Beatles

Pos **1** 1 Wks

YR	CH	40	10	RANK	GOLD	TITLE	SYM	TIME	ARTIST
58	21	17	15	516	O ●	Patricia [I]		2:28	Perez Prado
92	28	25	14	517	O ●	All 4 Love		3:30	Color Me Badd
80	27	22	14	518	O ●	Do That To Me One More Time		3:45	The Captain & Tennille
56	23	20	14	519	O	Hot Diggity (Dog Ziggity Boom)		2:19	Perry Como
57	28	22	13	520	O	Chances Are		3:00	Johnny Mathis
56	24	19	13	521	O	I Want You, I Need You, I Love You		2:37	Elvis Presley
64	22	19	13	522	O	Hello, Dolly!		2:22	Louis Armstrong
57	22	19	13	523	O	Don't Forbid Me		2:14	Pat Boone
57	21	17	13	524	O	Young Love		2:29	Sonny James
79	20	15	13	525	O	Still		3:43	Commodores
57	29	18	12	526	O	Diana		2:29	Paul Anka
58	21	18	12	527	O ●	Tom Dooley		3:01	The Kingston Trio
82	21	17	12	528	O ●	I Can't Go For That (No Can Do)		3:50	Daryl Hall & John Oates
58	23	16	12	529	O ●	Catch A Falling Star		2:25	Perry Como
58	17	14	12	530	O	Twilight Time		2:47	The Platters
80	26	18	11	531	O	Please Don't Go		3:43	K.C. & The Sunshine Band
59	20	17	11	532	O	Mr. Blue		2:18	The Fleetwoods
76	21	16	11	533	O	(Shake, Shake, Shake) Shake Your Booty		3:06	KC & The Sunshine Band
58	19	16	11	534	O	Little Star		2:37	The Elegants
62	21	15	11	535	O ●	Stranger On The Shore [I]		2:52	Mr. Acker Bilk
58	18	15	11	536	O	Bird Dog		2:12	The Everly Brothers
76	28	22	10	537	O ●	A Fifth Of Beethoven [I]		3:02	Walter Murphy/Big Apple Band
82	27	18	10	538	O ▲	Mickey		3:36	Toni Basil
81	26	17	10	539	O ●	The Tide Is High		3:50	Blondie
76	25	16	10	540	O ▲	Disco Duck (Part 1) [N]		3:15	Rick Dees & His Cast Of Idiots
78	22	16	10	541	O ●	If I Can't Have You		2:57	Yvonne Elliman
76	20	16	10	542	O ●	I Write The Songs		3:39	Barry Manilow
57	23	15	10	543	O	Party Doll		2:12	Buddy Knox/The Rhythm Orchids
69	17	15	10	544	O ●	Leaving On A Jet Plane		3:27	Peter, Paul & Mary
83	20	14	10	545	O ●	Let's Dance		4:08	David Bowie
75	17	14	10	546	O	One Of These Nights		3:28	Eagles
72	16	14	10	547	O ●	Brandy (You're A Fine Girl)		2:55	Looking Glass
76	16	14	10	548	O ●	Love Rollercoaster		2:52	Ohio Players
70	17	13	10	549	O ●	Make It With You		3:14	Bread
81	28	20	9	550	O ▲	Keep On Loving You		3:22	REO Speedwagon
79	24	20	9	551	O ●	Pop Muzik		3:20	M
79	27	19	9	552	O ●	Sad Eyes		3:30	Robert John
78	31	18	9	553	O ▲	Hot Child In The City		3:06	Nick Gilder
90	25	18	9	554	O ●	Hold On		3:32	Wilson Phillips

YR	WEEKS			RANK	G O L D	PEAK POSITION	PEAK WEEKS	S Y M	TIME	ARTIST
	CH	40	10							

Pos 1 1 Wks Cont'd

YR	CH	40	10	RANK	GOLD	TITLE	SYM	TIME	ARTIST
82	27	17	9	555	O	Who Can It Be Now?		3:20	Men At Work
83	26	17	9	556	O ●	Sweet Dreams (Are Made of This)		3:36	Eurythmics
91	24	17	9	557	O ●	More Than Words		4:05	Extreme
91	23	17	9	558	O ●	I Like The Way (The Kissing Game)		3:42	Hi-Five
91	25	16	9	559	O ▲	One More Try		3:24	Timmy -T-
78	24	16	9	560	O ▲	You're The One That I Want		2:49	John Travolta & Olivia Newton-John
84	24	16	9	561	O	Missing You		3:58	John Waite
91	23	16	9	562	O ●	Unbelievable		3:30	EMF
57	22	16	9	563	O ●	That'll Be The Day		2:14	The Crickets
85	21	16	9	564	O	Separate Lives		4:06	Phil Collins & Marilyn Martin
91	20	16	9	565	O	When A Man Loves A Woman		3:40	Michael Bolton
78	20	16	9	566	O ●	Miss You		3:31	The Rolling Stones
70	19	16	9	567	O	I Want You Back		2:44	The Jackson 5
74	18	16	9	568	O ●	Bennie And The Jets		5:10	Elton John
69	16	16	9	569	O ●	Come Together		4:16	The Beatles
82	28	15	9	570	O	Chariots Of Fire - Titles	[I]	3:15	Vangelis
71	22	15	9	571	O ●	Indian Reservation		2:55	Raiders
77	18	15	9	572	O	Got To Give It Up (Pt. I)		3:58	Marvin Gaye
69	16	15	9	573	O	Someday We'll Be Together		3:14	Diana Ross & The Supremes
72	16	15	9	574	O ●	Let's Stay Together		3:15	Al Green
58	16	15	9	575	O	Yakety Yak		1:50	The Coasters
77	23	14	9	576	O ▲	Car Wash		3:18	Rose Royce
85	21	14	9	577	O ●	Crazy For You		4:08	Madonna
92	20	14	9	578	O ●	This Used To Be My Playground		5:02	Madonna
79	20	14	9	579	O ●	What A Fool Believes		3:41	The Doobie Brothers
79	19	14	9	580	O ●	Good Times		3:42	Chic
67	16	14	9	581	O ●	Incense And Peppermints		2:37	Strawberry Alarm Clock
64	15	14	9	582	O	Mr. Lonely		2:37	Bobby Vinton
62	17	13	9	583	O	The Stripper	[I]	1:57	David Rose
79	15	13	9	584	O ●	Heartache Tonight		4:26	Eagles
70	14	13	9	585	O ●	Venus		3:05	The Shocking Blue
59	16	12	9	586	O	Why		2:30	Frankie Avalon
66	15	12	9	587	O ●	96 Tears		2:38	? & The Mysterians
66	15	12	9	588	O ●	Last Train To Clarksville		2:40	The Monkees
68	13	12	9	589	O ●	Harper Valley P.T.A.		3:12	Jeannie C. Riley
77	26	18	8	590	O ●	You Don't Have To Be A Star (To Be In My Show)		3:40	Marilyn McCoo & Billy Davis, Jr.
91	20	18	8	591	O ●	Set Adrift On Memory Bliss		3:53	PM Dawn
78	26	17	8	592	O ●	You Needed Me		3:38	Anne Murray
88	25	17	8	593	O	Need You Tonight		3:01	INXS
77	24	17	8	594	O	Don't Leave Me This Way		3:35	Thelma Houston
77	21	17	8	595	O ●	You Make Me Feel Like Dancing		2:48	Leo Sayer
87	22	16	8	596	O ▲	Shake You Down		4:04	Gregory Abbott
73	21	16	8	597	O	Touch Me In The Morning		3:51	Diana Ross
92	20	16	8	598	O ●	Don't Let The Sun Go Down On Me		5:44	George Michael/Elton John
74	20	16	8	599	O ●	The Joker		3:36	Steve Miller Band
85	23	15	8	600	O ●	Everytime You Go Away		4:10	Paul Young

♪ ♪ ♪ ♪ ♪ ♪

YR	CH	40	10	RANK	GOLD	TITLE	SYM	TIME	ARTIST
77	22	15	8	601	O ●	Dancing Queen		3:50	Abba
86	22	15	8	602	O	The Way It Is		4:57	Bruce Hornsby & The Range
88	22	15	8	603	O	Got My Mind Set On You		3:50	George Harrison
89	21	15	8	604	O ●	Cold Hearted		3:34	Paula Abdul
75	21	15	8	605	O ●	Before The Next Teardrop Falls		2:32	Freddy Fender
77	21	15	8	606	O ●	Southern Nights		2:58	Glen Campbell

bell.

DAWN's "Gypsy Rose" is comin' home...

THEIR CURRENT HIT SINGLE

"SAY, HAS ANYBODY SEEN MY SWEET GYPSY ROSE"

RECORDED BY   FEATURING

DAWN   TONY ORLANDO

Written by IRWIN LEVINE & L. RUSSELL BROWN
Produced by HANK MEDRESS, DAVE APPELL and THE TOKENS

on Bell #45,374

BELL RECORDS
A Division of Columbia Pictures Industries, Inc.

YR	WEEKS			RANK	G O L D	PEAK POSITION	PEAK WEEKS	S Y M	TIME	ARTIST
	CH	40	10							

Pos **1** **1** Wks Cont'd

YR	CH	40	10	RANK	GOLD	TITLE	TIME	ARTIST
77	20	15	8	607	O ●	Blinded By The Light	3:48	Manfred Mann's Earth Band
77	19	15	8	608	O ●	Hotel California	6:08	Eagles
74	19	15	8	609	O ●	Then Came You	3:53	Dionne Warwicke & Spinners
77	17	15	8	610	O ●	I Wish	3:37	Stevie Wonder
75	23	14	8	611	O ●	My Eyes Adored You	3:25	Frankie Valli
85	22	14	8	612	O	Don't You (Forget About Me)	4:20	Simple Minds
72	22	14	8	613	O ●	I Am Woman	3:04	Helen Reddy
81	21	14	8	614	O ●	Stars on 45	4:05	Stars on 45
85	21	14	8	615	O	Part-Time Lover	3:43	Stevie Wonder
90	21	14	8	616	O ▲	Blaze Of Glory	5:30	Jon Bon Jovi
73	20	14	8	617	O ●	Delta Dawn	3:08	Helen Reddy
90	19	14	8	618	O ●	I'm Your Baby Tonight	4:54	Whitney Houston
88	19	14	8	619	O	So Emotional	3:46	Whitney Houston
81	19	14	8	620	O ●	The One That You Love	4:07	Air Supply
72	15	14	8	621	O	I'll Take You There	3:19	The Staple Singers
77	20	13	8	622	O ●	Gonna Fly Now	[I] 2:45	Bill Conti
89	18	13	8	623	O ●	Don't Wanna Lose You	4:10	Gloria Estefan
75	18	13	8	624	O ●	Lovin' You	3:20	Minnie Riperton
71	16	13	8	625	O ●	Want Ads	2:34	The Honey Cone
64	15	13	8	626	O ●	Everybody Loves Somebody	2:40	Dean Martin
60	15	13	8	627	O	Itsy Bitsy Teenie Weenie Yellow Polkadot Bikini	[N] 2:19	Brian Hyland
72	14	13	8	628	O	Heart Of Gold	2:59	Neil Young
60	15	12	8	629	O	Alley-Oop	[N] 2:36	Hollywood Argyles
61	14	12	8	630	O	Mother-In-Law	2:25	Ernie K-Doe
71	14	12	8	631	O ●	You've Got A Friend	4:26	James Taylor
78	18	11	8	632	O ●	Too Much, Too Little, Too Late	3:00	Johnny Mathis/Deniece Williams
65	13	11	8	633	O	My Girl	2:55	The Temptations
64	12	11	8	634	O	A World Without Love	2:38	Peter & Gordon
91	20	19	7	635	O	Romantic	3:48	Karyn White
90	30	17	7	636	O ●	Close To You	3:55	Maxi Priest
77	25	17	7	637	O ●	Undercover Angel	3:24	Alan O'Day
88	27	16	7	638	O ●	Wild, Wild West	3:59	The Escape Club
74	22	16	7	639	O ●	Love's Theme	[I] 3:30	Love Unlimited Orchestra
74	22	16	7	640	O ●	Show And Tell	3:28	Al Wilson
89	29	15	7	641	O ▲	Wind Beneath My Wings	4:54	Bette Midler
85	27	15	7	642	O	Take On Me	3:46	a-ha
90	26	15	7	643	O	I Don't Have The Heart	3:52	James Ingram
89	24	15	7	644	O ●	My Prerogative	4:25	Bobby Brown
61	23	15	7	645	O	Please Mr. Postman	2:20	The Marvelettes
91	22	15	7	646	O	Love Will Never Do (Without You)	4:26	Janet Jackson
85	22	15	7	647	O	Saving All My Love For You	3:48	Whitney Houston
90	21	15	7	648	O ▲	Ice Ice Baby	4:53	Vanilla Ice
76	21	15	7	649	O ●	Boogie Fever	3:25	Sylvers
91	20	15	7	650	O ●	Good Vibrations	4:26	Marky Mark & The Funky Bunch
86	20	15	7	651	O	Human	3:46	Human League
75	20	15	7	652	O ●	Laughter In The Rain	2:50	Neil Sedaka
83	18	15	7	653	O	Tell Her About It	3:35	Billy Joel
87	28	14	7	654	O	Here I Go Again	3:52	Whitesnake
90	26	14	7	655	O ●	(Can't Live Without Your) Love And Affection	3:47	Nelson
89	23	14	7	656	O ●	She Drives Me Crazy	3:35	Fine Young Cannibals
86	22	14	7	657	O ●	Addicted To Love	3:59	Robert Palmer
87	22	14	7	658	O	Always	3:59	Atlantic Starr
79	21	14	7	659	O ●	Heart Of Glass	3:22	Blondie

YR	WEEKS CH	40	10	RANK	G O L D	PEAK POSITION	PEAK WEEKS	S Y M	TIME	ARTIST

Pos 1 ¹ Wks Cont'd

YR	CH	40	10	RANK	GOLD	TITLE			TIME	ARTIST
86	21	14	7	660	O	There'll Be Sad Songs (To Make You Cry)			4:02	Billy Ocean
86	21	14	7	661	O	Sledgehammer			4:58	Peter Gabriel
86	20	14	7	662	O	West End Girls			3:55	Pet Shop Boys
77	20	14	7	663	O ●	When I Need You			4:11	Leo Sayer
87	20	14	7	664	O ●	Head To Toe			3:58	Lisa Lisa & Cult Jam
73	20	14	7	665	O ●	Frankenstein		[I]	3:28	The Edgar Winter Group
74	19	14	7	666	O	You Haven't Done Nothin			3:20	Stevie Wonder
91	19	14	7	667	O	You're In Love			3:58	Wilson Phillips
87	18	14	7	668	O	Shakedown			3:59	Bob Seger
74	18	14	7	669	O ●	Nothing From Nothing			2:40	Billy Preston
75	18	14	7	670	O ●	(Hey Won't You Play) Another Somebody Done Somebody Wrong Song			3:23	B.J. Thomas
59	17	14	7	671	O	The Happy Organ		[I]	2:01	Dave 'Baby' Cortez
74	17	14	7	672	O ●	Hooked On A Feeling			2:54	Blue Swede
70	15	14	7	673	O ●	Cracklin' Rosie			2:47	Neil Diamond
72	15	14	7	674	O	Oh Girl			3:16	Chi-Lites
85	22	13	7	675	O	Miami Vice Theme		[I]	2:26	Jan Hammer
86	21	13	7	676	O ●	Take My Breath Away			4:13	Berlin
80	21	13	7	677	O ●	Sailing			4:15	Christopher Cross
90	20	13	7	678	O	If Wishes Came True			5:09	Sweet Sensation
86	20	13	7	679	O	Sara			4:18	Starship
77	19	13	7	680	O ●	Don't Give Up On Us			3:30	David Soul
89	19	13	7	681	O ●	The Look			3:56	Roxette
77	19	13	7	682	O ●	Dreams			4:14	Fleetwood Mac
74	18	13	7	683	O ●	Sunshine On My Shoulders			3:18	John Denver
74	18	13	7	684	O ●	Band On The Run			5:09	Paul McCartney & Wings
75	18	13	7	685	O	Lady Marmalade			3:14	LaBelle
73	17	13	7	686	O	You Are The Sunshine Of My Life			2:45	Stevie Wonder
75	17	13	7	687	O ●	Pick Up The Pieces		[I]	3:00	AWB (Average White Band)
76	17	13	7	688	O	Theme From Mahogany (Do You Know Where You're Going To)			3:19	Diana Ross
73	16	13	7	689	O ●	Angie			4:30	The Rolling Stones
77	15	13	7	690	O ●	New Kid In Town			4:49	Eagles
77	22	12	7	691	O ●	Da Doo Ron Ron			2:46	Shaun Cassidy
76	20	12	7	692	O ●	You Should Be Dancing			4:15	Bee Gees
86	19	12	7	693	O	Venus			3:49	Bananarama
76	19	12	7	694	O	Let Your Love Flow			3:16	Bellamy Brothers
75	19	12	7	695	O ●	The Hustle		[I]	3:27	Van McCoy
75	17	12	7	696	O ●	Black Water			4:17	The Doobie Brothers
62	16	12	7	697	O	The Loco-Motion			2:12	Little Eva
61	16	12	7	698	O	Wooden Heart			2:00	Joe Dowell
74	15	12	7	699	O ●	You're Sixteen			2:50	Ringo Starr
75	15	12	7	700	O ●	Let's Do It Again			3:28	The Staple Singers
66	15	12	7	701	O	Poor Side Of Town			3:03	Johnny Rivers
63	15	12	7	702	O	So Much In Love			2:08	The Tymes
63	15	12	7	703	O	Deep Purple			2:41	Nino Tempo & April Stevens
66	14	12	7	704	O ●	These Boots Are Made For Walkin'			2:40	Nancy Sinatra
66	14	12	7	705	O ●	Good Vibrations			3:35	The Beach Boys
66	14	12	7	706	O	Good Lovin'			2:28	The Young Rascals
71	13	12	7	707	O ●	Uncle Albert/Admiral Halsey			4:47	Paul & Linda McCartney
68	13	12	7	708	O ●	Green Tambourine			2:22	The Lemon Pipers
74	18	11	7	709	O ●	Sundown			3:37	Gordon Lightfoot
72	16	11	7	710	O	Ben			2:42	Michael Jackson

YR	WEEKS			RANK	G O L D	PEAK POSITION	PEAK WEEKS	S Y M	TIME	ARTIST
	CH	40	10							
						Pos **1** 1 Wks Cont'd				
75	16	11	7	711	O ●	Have You Never Been Mellow			3:28	Olivia Newton-John
76	16	11	7	712	O ●	Convoy	[N]		3:48	C.W. McCall
66	15	11	7	713	O	Strangers In The Night			2:35	Frank Sinatra
75	14	11	7	714	O ●	Listen To What The Man Said			3:53	Wings
76	14	11	7	715	O ●	Welcome Back			2:48	John Sebastian
73	14	11	7	716	O	Give Me Love - (Give Me Peace On Earth)			3:32	George Harrison
65	14	11	7	717	O	Hang On Sloopy			2:57	The McCoys
60	13	10	7	718	O	Mr. Custer	[N]		2:59	Larry Verne
66	13	10	7	719	O	Sunshine Superman			3:11	Donovan
65	13	10	7	720	O	Mr. Tambourine Man			2:18	The Byrds
64	12	10	7	721	O	Ringo	[S]		3:00	Lorne Greene
67	11	10	7	722	O	Love Is Here And Now You're Gone			2:35	The Supremes
65	11	10	7	723	O	Eve Of Destruction			3:28	Barry McGuire
67	12	9	7	724	O ●	Ruby Tuesday			3:12	The Rolling Stones
67	11	9	7	725	O ●	All You Need Is Love			3:57	The Beatles
76	28	19	6	726	O	Love Machine (Part 1)			2:55	The Miracles
88	40	16	6	727	O ●	Red Red Wine	[R]		5:21	UB40
77	23	16	6	728	O	I'm Your Boogie Man			3:58	KC & The Sunshine Band
83	21	16	6	729	O ●	Africa			4:23	Toto
88	20	16	6	730	O	Seasons Change			3:58	Expose
88	25	15	6	731	O ●	Wishing Well			3:33	Terence Trent D'Arby
88	24	15	6	732	O ●	Baby, I Love Your Way/Freebird Medley (Free Baby)			4:07	Will To Power
89	22	15	6	733	O ●	If You Don't Know Me By Now			3:24	Simply Red
87	21	15	6	734	O	Heaven Is A Place On Earth			3:49	Belinda Carlisle
87	21	15	6	735	O ●	(I've Had) The Time Of My Life			4:47	Bill Medley & Jennifer Warnes
86	21	15	6	736	O	The Next Time I Fall			3:43	Peter Cetera w/Amy Grant
90	20	15	6	737	O ●	Love Will Lead You Back			4:18	Taylor Dayne
86	24	14	6	738	O	You Give Love A Bad Name			3:53	Bon Jovi
83	23	14	6	739	O	Come On Eileen			4:12	Dexys Midnight Runners
86	23	14	6	740	O	Holding Back The Years			4:04	Simply Red
86	22	14	6	741	O	Higher Love			4:08	Steve Winwood
89	22	14	6	742	O	Listen To Your Heart			5:26	Roxette
89	21	14	6	743	O ●	I'll Be Loving You (Forever)			3:54	New Kids On The Block
88	21	14	6	744	O	Hold On To The Nights			4:34	Richard Marx
89	21	14	6	745	O ●	Baby Don't Forget My Number			4:01	Milli Vanilli
79	20	14	6	746	O ▲	Knock On Wood			3:40	Amii Stewart
89	20	14	6	747	O	The Living Years			5:30	Mike & The Mechanics
88	20	14	6	748	O	Foolish Beat			4:20	Debbie Gibson
91	19	14	6	749	O ●	I've Been Thinking About You			3:40	Londonbeat
75	19	14	6	750	O	Best Of My Love			3:25	The Eagles
89	19	14	6	751	O ●	Eternal Flame			3:56	Bangles
87	18	14	6	752	O	Open Your Heart			4:12	Madonna
85	17	14	6	753	O ●	Sussudio			4:23	Phil Collins
88	23	13	6	754	O	Love Bites			5:46	Def Leppard
89	22	13	6	755	O	I'll Be There For You			5:43	Bon Jovi
85	21	13	6	756	O	Oh Sheila			3:36	Ready For The World
87	21	13	6	757	O	You Keep Me Hangin' On			4:13	Kim Wilde
86	20	13	6	758	O	These Dreams			3:46	Heart
87	20	13	6	759	O ●	Lost In Emotion			3:59	Lisa Lisa & Cult Jam
91	19	13	6	760	O	Joyride			3:53	Roxette
74	18	13	6	761	O ●	Rock Me Gently			3:28	Andy Kim
86	18	13	6	762	O	Live To Tell			4:37	Madonna
88	18	13	6	763	O	The Way You Make Me Feel			4:26	Michael Jackson
74	17	13	6	764	O ●	Angie Baby			3:29	Helen Reddy

YR	WEEKS			RANK	G O L D	PEAK POSITION	PEAK WEEKS		S Y M	TIME	ARTIST
	CH	40	10								

YR	CH	40	10	RANK		TITLE		SYM	TIME	ARTIST
73	17	13	6	765	O ●	We're An American Band			3:25	Grand Funk
89	17	13	6	766	O	Good Thing			3:22	Fine Young Cannibals
73	16	13	6	767	O	Superstition			3:59	Stevie Wonder
74	16	13	6	768	O ●	Feel Like Makin' Love			2:55	Roberta Flack
60	15	13	6	769	O	I Want To Be Wanted			3:00	Brenda Lee
69	15	13	6	770	O ●	Suspicious Minds			4:22	Elvis Presley
73	14	13	6	771	O ●	Love Train			2:59	O'Jays
76	24	12	6	772	O ●	Theme From S.W.A.T.	[I]		2:47	Rhythm Heritage
87	22	12	6	773		Mony Mony "Live"			4:00	Billy Idol
79	21	12	6	774	O ▲	Don't Stop 'Til You Get Enough			5:45	Michael Jackson
74	19	12	6	775	O ●	Cat's In The Cradle			3:29	Harry Chapin
88	18	12	6	776	O	Together Forever			3:20	Rick Astley
76	17	12	6	777	O ●	Saturday Night			2:56	Bay City Rollers
86	17	12	6	778	O	Invisible Touch			3:26	Genesis
75	17	12	6	779	O ●	Fallin' In Love			3:13	Hamilton, Joe Frank & Reynolds
89	17	12	6	780	O ▲	Hangin' Tough			3:51	New Kids On The Block
73	16	12	6	781	O ●	Photograph			3:59	Ringo Starr
74	16	12	6	782	O ●	Dark Lady			3:26	Cher
72	16	12	6	783	O ●	Papa Was A Rollin' Stone			6:58	The Temptations
61	15	12	6	784	O	Moody River			2:38	Pat Boone
87	15	12	6	785	O	Jacob's Ladder			3:28	Huey Lewis & the News
72	13	12	6	786	O ●	Song Sung Blue			3:15	Neil Diamond
89	18	11	6	787	O ▲	Batdance			4:06	Prince
74	17	11	6	788	O ●	The Night Chicago Died			3:30	Paper Lace
87	16	11	6	789	O	Who's That Girl			3:58	Madonna
64	14	11	6	790	O	Love Me Do			2:18	The Beatles
87	14	11	6	791	O ●	I Just Can't Stop Loving You			4:17	Michael Jackson
65	12	11	6	792	O	Over And Over			2:00	The Dave Clark Five
66	15	10	6	793	O ●	Lightnin' Strikes			2:44	Lou Christie
90	14	10	6	794	O	Praying For Time			4:30	George Michael
63	13	10	6	795	O	Our Day Will Come			2:31	Ruby & The Romantics
62	13	10	6	796	O	Don't Break The Heart That Loves You			2:58	Connie Francis
67	11	10	6	797	O	The Happening			2:50	The Supremes
65	11	9	6	798	O	Ticket To Ride			3:02	The Beatles
65	10	8	6	799	O ●	I'm Henry VIII, I Am			1:49	Herman's Hermits
88	28	15	5	800	O ▲	Kokomo			3:34	The Beach Boys

♪ ♪ ♪ ♪ ♪ ♪

YR	CH	40	10	RANK		TITLE		SYM	TIME	ARTIST
75	19	15	5	801	O ●	Thank God I'm A Country Boy			2:47	John Denver
75	20	14	5	802	O ●	Shining Star			2:50	Earth, Wind & Fire
76	18	14	5	803	O	Rock'n Me			3:05	Steve Miller
60	18	14	5	804	O	Stay			1:50	Maurice Williams & The Zodiacs
89	28	13	5	805	O ●	When I'm With You	[R]		3:54	Sheriff
89	21	13	5	806	O ●	Rock On			3:21	Michael Damian
77	19	13	5	807	O ●	Looks Like We Made It			3:29	Barry Manilow
79	19	13	5	808	O ●	Love You Inside Out			3:48	Bee Gees
90	18	13	5	809	O ●	I'll Be Your Everything			3:58	Tommy Page
91	16	13	5	810	O	The Promise Of A New Day			4:09	Paula Abdul
89	15	13	5	811	O	Satisfied			3:58	Richard Marx
74	17	12	5	812	O ●	You Ain't Seen Nothing Yet			3:29	Bachman-Turner Overdrive
75	17	12	5	813	O ●	Please Mr. Postman			2:48	Carpenters
75	16	12	5	814	O ●	Mandy			3:15	Barry Manilow
90	16	12	5	815	O ●	Black Cat			4:25	Janet Jackson
88	14	11	5	816	O	Dirty Diana			4:37	Michael Jackson
74	18	10	5	817	O ●	Rock The Boat			3:03	The Hues Corporation
75	16	10	5	818	O	You're No Good			3:40	Linda Ronstadt

YR	WEEKS CH	40	10	RANK	GOLD	PEAK POSITION	TIME	ARTIST

Pos 1 · 1 Wks Cont'd

YR	CH	40	10	RANK			TIME	ARTIST
74	14	10	5	819	O ●	I Shot The Sheriff	3:30	Eric Clapton
60	13	10	5	820	O	Georgia On My Mind	3:37	Ray Charles
64	12	10	5	821	O	Leader Of The Pack	2:48	The Shangri-Las
65	11	10	5	822	O	Game Of Love	2:04	Wayne Fontana/The Mindbenders
65	11	10	5	823	O	Back In My Arms Again	2:50	The Supremes
72	11	9	5	824	O ●	Black & White	3:24	Three Dog Night
67	10	9	5	825	O ●	Penny Lane	3:00	The Beatles
61	17	15	4	826	O	Running Scared	2:10	Roy Orbison
75	18	13	4	827	O ●	I'm Sorry	3:29	John Denver
75	17	12	4	828	O ●	Fire	3:12	Ohio Players
75	16	12	4	829	O	Sister Golden Hair	3:16	America
75	15	9	4	830	O	Get Down Tonight	3:06	K.C. & The Sunshine Band
74	12	9	4	831	O ●	Can't Get Enough Of Your Love, Babe	3:15	Barry White
74	15	11	3	832	O	Whatever Gets You Thru The Night	3:20	John Lennon/Plastic Ono Band

Pos 2 · 10 Wks

YR	CH	40	10	RANK			TIME	ARTIST
81	23	19	15	833	O ●	Waiting For A Girl Like You	4:35	Foreigner

Pos 2 · 8 Wks

YR	CH	40	10	RANK			TIME	ARTIST
92	27	24	15	834	O ▲	If I Ever Fall In Love	3:05	Shai
57	26	21	10	835	O	Little Darlin'	2:05	The Diamonds

Pos 2 · 6 Wks

YR	CH	40	10	RANK			TIME	ARTIST
55	25	25	19	836	O	Moments To Remember	3:14	The Four Lads
92	33	24	15	837	O ▲	Baby-Baby-Baby	4:05	TLC
92	24	20	11	838	O ●	Sometimes Love Just Ain't Enough	4:26	Patty Smyth with Don Henley
82	18	14	10	839	O	Open Arms	3:21	Journey
78	20	15	9	840	O ●	Baker Street	4:08	Gerry Rafferty
63	18	13	9	841	O	Louie Louie	2:24	The Kingsmen

Pos 2 · 5 Wks

YR	CH	40	10	RANK			TIME	ARTIST
82	23	18	11	842	O ●	Rosanna	3:59	Toto
62	16	14	10	843	O ●	Return To Sender	2:05	Elvis Presley
80	23	15	9	844	O ●	More Than I Can Say	3:40	Leo Sayer
83	22	15	8	845	O ▲	Electric Avenue	3:47	Eddy Grant

Pos 2 · 4 Wks

YR	CH	40	10	RANK			TIME	ARTIST
57	38	26	18	846	O	So Rare	2:30	Jimmy Dorsey
82	28	22	16	847	O ●	Hurts So Good	3:35	John Cougar
57	27	22	15	848	O	Bye Bye Love	2:17	The Everly Brothers
92	26	23	12	849	O ▲	Tears In Heaven	4:29	Eric Clapton
56	24	19	12	850	O	No, Not Much!	3:12	The Four Lads
91	22	19	11	851	O ●	It's So Hard To Say Goodbye To Yesterday	2:45	Boyz II Men
56	21	17	11	852	O	Blue Suede Shoes	2:14	Carl Perkins
82	21	16	11	853	O	Don't Talk To Strangers	3:00	Rick Springfield
80	27	17	10	854	O ●	All Out Of Love	3:41	Air Supply
91	23	16	10	855	O ▲	I Wanna Sex You Up	4:09	Color Me Badd
60	20	15	10	856	O	Last Date [I]	2:20	Floyd Cramer
83	18	15	10	857	O	Say It Isn't So	3:56	Daryl Hall - John Oates
80	21	17	9	858	O	Ride Like The Wind	3:54	Christopher Cross
84	21	15	9	859	O ▲	Dancing In The Dark	3:59	Bruce Springsteen
60	20	15	9	860	O	Greenfields	3:00	The Brothers Four

YR	CH	40	10	RANK	GOLD	PEAK POSITION		SYM	TIME	ARTIST

Pos 2 — 4 Wks Cont'd

YR	CH	40	10	RANK	GOLD	TITLE		SYM	TIME	ARTIST
70	17	14	9	861	O •	We've Only Just Begun			3:09	Carpenters
58	21	13	9	862	O	Great Balls Of Fire			1:50	Jerry Lee Lewis
83	21	19	8	863	O	Shame On The Moon			4:55	Bob Seger/The Silver Bullet Band
84	18	14	8	864	O •	The Wild Boys			4:14	Duran Duran
66	12	11	8	865	O •	Snoopy Vs. The Red Baron	[N]		2:43	The Royal Guardsmen
64	26	16	7	866	O	Twist And Shout			2:33	The Beatles
63	15	12	7	867	O	Can't Get Used To Losing You			2:19	Andy Williams
68	13	11	7	868	O	(Theme From) Valley Of The Dolls			3:35	Dionne Warwick
87	19	14	6	869	O	Looking For A New Love			3:58	Jody Watley
73	14	11	6	870	O •	Dueling Banjos	[I]		3:17	Eric Weissberg & Steve Mandell
75	10	7	5	871	O	Calypso			3:32	John Denver

Pos 2 — 3 Wks

YR	CH	40	10	RANK	GOLD	TITLE		SYM	TIME	ARTIST
56	39	22	16	872	O	Honky Tonk (Parts 1 & 2)	[I]		5:35	Bill Doggett
57	27	21	16	873	O	Blueberry Hill			2:14	Fats Domino
92	28	23	15	874	O ▲	Rump Shaker			3:51	Wreckx-N-Effect
56	27	22	15	875	O	Whatever Will Be, Will Be (Que Sera, Sera)			2:01	Doris Day
55	18	17	14	876	O	I Hear You Knocking			2:20	Gale Storm
92	30	22	13	877	O •	My Lovin' (You're Never Gonna Get It)			4:32	En Vogue
79	26	20	12	878	O ▲	Y.M.C.A.			3:30	Village People
60	23	20	12	879	O	He'll Have To Go			2:16	Jim Reeves
81	20	17	12	880	O •	Woman			3:30	John Lennon
92	26	21	11	881	O	I Love Your Smile			4:19	Shanice
81	24	19	11	882	O	Start Me Up			3:32	The Rolling Stones
81	24	16	11	883	O •	Slow Hand			3:57	Pointer Sisters
81	24	16	11	884	O	Just The Two Of Us			3:40	Grover Washington, Jr. with Bill Withers
59	18	14	11	885	O	Put Your Head On My Shoulder			2:39	Paul Anka
82	36	22	10	886	O •	Gloria			4:50	Laura Branigan
77	26	18	10	887	O •	Don't It Make My Brown Eyes Blue			2:37	Crystal Gayle
81	20	17	10	888	O	Love On The Rocks			3:41	Neil Diamond
81	25	16	10	889	O •	Being With You			3:58	Smokey Robinson
59	19	14	10	890	O	Personality			2:35	Lloyd Price
83	18	14	10	891	O •	The Girl Is Mine			3:41	Michael Jackson/Paul McCartney
83	25	18	9	892	O	Do You Really Want To Hurt Me			4:23	Culture Club
83	25	17	9	893	O •	Making Love Out Of Nothing At All			4:29	Air Supply
76	21	17	9	894	O •	The Rubberband Man			3:30	Spinners
76	21	15	9	895	O •	Get Up And Boogie (That's Right)			4:05	Silver Convention
82	19	15	9	896	O	We Got The Beat			2:30	Go-Go's
85	22	14	9	897	O ▲	Party All The Time			3:58	Eddie Murphy
67	17	14	9	898	O	I Heard It Through The Grapevine			2:52	Gladys Knight & The Pips
69	15	12	9	899	O	Crystal Blue Persuasion			3:45	Tommy James
77	25	15	8	900	O •	Nobody Does It Better			3:30	Carly Simon
76	20	14	8	901	O •	Dream Weaver			3:15	Gary Wright
58	20	14	8	902	O	26 Miles (Santa Catalina)			2:31	The Four Preps
84	19	14	8	903	O •	Somebody's Watching Me			3:57	Rockwell
58	18	14	8	904	O	Stood Up			1:57	Ricky Nelson
68	15	13	8	905	O •	Young Girl			3:12	Union Gap feat. Gary Puckett
71	15	13	8	906	O	What's Going On			3:40	Marvin Gaye
61	16	12	8	907	O	The Boll Weevil Song	[N]		2:35	Brook Benton
59	15	12	8	908	O	Charlie Brown	[N]		2:12	The Coasters
67	15	11	8	909	O •	Soul Man			2:36	Sam & Dave
85	25	15	7	910	O •	Cherish			3:58	Kool & The Gang

YR	CH	40	10	RANK	GOLD	PEAK POSITION	TIME	ARTIST

Pos 2 — 3 Wks Cont'd

YR	CH	40	10	RANK	GOLD	TITLE	TIME	ARTIST
77	20	14	7	911	O	Keep It Comin' Love	3:48	KC & The Sunshine Band
73	17	14	7	912	O ●	Goodbye Yellow Brick Road	3:13	Elton John
68	14	12	7	913	O ●	Those Were The Days	5:05	Mary Hopkin
69	14	12	7	914	O ▲	Proud Mary	3:07	Creedence Clearwater Revival
73	14	12	7	915	O ●	Live And Let Die	3:10	Wings
69	13	12	7	916	O ●	Spinning Wheel	2:39	Blood, Sweat & Tears
58	16	11	7	917	O	Sweet Little Sixteen	2:35	Chuck Berry
69	12	11	7	918	O ●	A Boy Named Sue [N]	3:40	Johnny Cash
71	12	11	7	919	O	Never Can Say Goodbye	2:56	The Jackson 5
61	17	10	7	920	O	I Like It Like That, Part 1	1:55	Chris Kenner
66	12	10	7	921	O ●	Mellow Yellow	3:40	Donovan
90	21	14	6	922	O ●	Don't Wanna Fall In Love	4:04	Jane Child
76	19	14	6	923	O ●	All By Myself	4:22	Eric Carmen
89	20	13	6	924	O ▲	On Our Own	4:30	Bobby Brown
77	20	13	6	925	O	I'm In You	3:57	Peter Frampton
88	19	13	6	926	O	Shattered Dreams	3:30	Johnny Hates Jazz
86	16	12	6	927	O	Typical Male	4:14	Tina Turner
68	14	12	6	928	O ●	The Horse [I]	2:25	Cliff Nobles & Co.
68	13	12	6	929	O ●	Born To Be Wild	2:55	Steppenwolf
81	16	11	6	930	O	All Those Years Ago	3:42	George Harrison
65	15	11	6	931	O ●	A Lover's Concerto	2:36	The Toys
63	13	11	6	932	O	Ruby Baby	2:31	Dion
69	13	11	6	933	O ●	You've Made Me So Very Happy	3:26	Blood, Sweat & Tears
63	13	10	6	934	O	Be My Baby	2:20	The Ronettes
66	10	9	6	935	O	19th Nervous Breakdown	3:50	The Rolling Stones
67	10	9	6	936	O	Dedicated To The One I Love	2:56	Mamas & The Papas
63	10	8	6	937	O	Hello Mudduh, Hello Fadduh! (A Letter From Camp) [C]	2:47	Allan Sherman
78	20	13	5	938	O ●	Short People [N]	2:54	Randy Newman
87	18	11	5	939	O	Causing A Commotion	4:00	Madonna
75	17	11	5	940	O	I'm Not In Love	3:40	10cc
64	13	10	5	941	O	You Don't Own Me	2:26	Lesley Gore

Pos 2 — 2 Wks

YR	CH	40	10	RANK	GOLD	TITLE	TIME	ARTIST
56	31	23	14	942	O	Canadian Sunset [I]	2:50	Hugo Winterhalter/Eddie Heywood
56	27	22	12	943	O	Allegheny Moon	2:48	Patti Page
62	23	17	12	944	O	Limbo Rock	2:22	Chubby Checker
81	27	19	10	945	O ●	Queen Of Hearts	3:29	Juice Newton
58	21	19	10	946	O	Rock-in Robin	2:25	Bobby Day
81	26	18	10	947	O ●	Theme From "Greatest American Hero" (Believe It or Not)	3:11	Joey Scarbury
59	23	18	10	948	O	Donna	2:20	Ritchie Valens
76	24	17	10	949	O ●	I'd Really Love To See You Tonight	2:36	England Dan & John Ford Coley
72	21	16	10	950	O ●	I Gotcha	2:18	Joe Tex
70	19	15	10	951	O ▲	One Less Bell To Answer	3:29	The 5th Dimension
57	19	14	10	952	O	Love Me	2:39	Elvis Presley
77	27	17	9	953	O ▲	Boogie Nights	3:36	Heatwave
90	24	16	9	954	O ▲	Pump Up The Jam	3:36	Technotronic Featuring Felly
74	22	16	9	955	O	Dancing Machine	2:29	The Jackson 5
62	18	15	9	956	O	Mashed Potato Time	2:27	Dee Dee Sharp
79	21	14	9	957	O ●	Dim All The Lights	3:55	Donna Summer
65	18	14	9	958	O ●	Wooly Bully	2:20	Sam The Sham & the Pharoahs
61	16	14	9	959	O	Bristol Stomp	2:18	The Dovells
83	18	13	9	960	O	Time (Clock Of The Heart)	3:41	Culture Club

YR	CH	40	10	RANK	G O L D	PEAK POSITION	PEAK WEEKS	S Y M	TIME	ARTIST

Pos **2** **2** Wks Cont'd

YR	CH	40	10	RANK	GOLD	Title	TIME	ARTIST
79	17	13	9	961	O ●	After The Love Has Gone	3:55	Earth, Wind & Fire
67	16	13	9	962	O ●	Little Bit O'Soul	2:18	The Music Explosion
91	21	19	8	963	O	Do Anything	3:57	Natural Selection
89	26	16	8	964	O ●	Don't Know Much	3:33	Linda Ronstadt feat. Aaron Neville
80	25	16	8	965	O ●	Working My Way Back To You/Forgive Me, Girl	4:01	Spinners
79	23	16	8	966	O ●	Fire	3:41	Pointer Sisters
73	23	15	8	967	O ●	Playground In My Mind	2:55	Clint Holmes
76	20	15	8	968	O ●	Right Back Where We Started From	3:16	Maxine Nightingale
84	25	14	8	969	O ▲	Girls Just Want To Have Fun	3:55	Cyndi Lauper
74	25	14	8	970	O ●	You Make Me Feel Brand New	4:45	The Stylistics
59	21	14	8	971	O	16 Candles	2:49	The Crests
78	20	14	8	972	O ●	The Closer I Get To You	4:39	Roberta Flack with Donny Hathaway
86	17	14	8	973	O	Dancing On The Ceiling	4:20	Lionel Richie
76	21	13	8	974	O ●	You'll Never Find Another Love Like Mine	3:36	Lou Rawls
90	20	13	8	975	O ●	All I Wanna Do Is Make Love To You	4:24	Heart
60	16	13	8	976	O	Chain Gang	2:32	Sam Cooke
71	16	13	8	977	O	Mr. Big Stuff	2:27	Jean Knight
62	16	13	8	978	O	Ramblin' Rose	2:45	Nat King Cole
69	15	13	8	979	O ●	Hair	3:28	The Cowsills
72	15	13	8	980	O ●	Long Cool Woman (In A Black Dress)	3:02	The Hollies
67	16	12	8	981	O ●	The Rain, The Park & Other Things	2:57	The Cowsills
67	16	12	8	982	O ●	Georgy Girl	2:20	The Seekers
71	13	12	8	983	O ●	Superstar	3:49	Carpenters
69	13	12	8	984	O	I'm Gonna Make You Love Me	2:56	Supremes & Temptations
72	14	11	8	985	O ●	Too Late To Turn Back Now	3:12	Cornelius Brothers & Sister Rose
67	14	11	8	986	O ●	Never My Love	2:49	The Association
68	14	11	8	987	O ●	For Once In My Life	2:49	Stevie Wonder
72	13	11	8	988	O	Rockin' Robin	2:30	Michael Jackson
76	27	18	7	989	O	Love Is Alive	3:24	Gary Wright
87	23	16	7	990	O	C'est La Vie	3:28	Robbie Nevil
85	23	16	7	991	O ●	Easy Lover	4:40	Philip Bailey/Phil Collins
80	23	16	7	992	O ●	Yes, I'm Ready	3:05	Teri DeSario with K.C.
86	21	15	7	993	O	Everybody Have Fun Tonight	3:59	Wang Chung
86	21	14	7	994	O	Friends And Lovers	3:50	Gloria Loring & Carl Anderson
89	19	14	7	995	O ●	Heaven	3:58	Warrant
76	18	14	7	996	O ●	Love To Love You Baby	4:57	Donna Summer
74	18	14	7	997	O ●	Do It ('Til You're Satisfied)	3:09	B.T. Express
59	18	14	7	998	O	My Happiness	2:28	Connie Francis
72	18	14	7	999	O ●	Nights In White Satin	4:20	The Moody Blues
72	16	14	7	1000	O ●	Clair	3:00	Gilbert O'Sullivan

Eddie Kendricks' Keep On Truckin' is movin' out.

Eddie Kendricks' newest single, Keep On Truckin' was released
just a week ago, and it's already sold over
a quarter-million copies. That's truckin'.
Eddie Kendricks. Keep On Truckin'. Motown Single #T54238FA

©1973 Motown Record Corporation

#T327L

Snuff Garrett added
new brilliance to our logo...

"the night the
lights went out
in georgia"

recorded by

vicki lawrence

Our First Release From
SNUFF GARRETT MUSIC ENTERPRISES
on Bell # 45.303

BELL RECORDS,
A Division of Columbia Pictures Industries, Inc.

THE
YEARS

This section lists, in rank order, the Top 40 hits year-by-year. The ranking is based on the *Top 1000* ranking system.

You will note, in order to round out the Top 40 records of each year, several hundred additional hits are listed which do not appear in the *Top 1000*.

Columnar headings show the following data:

PK DATE: Date record reached its peak position
PK WKS: Total weeks record held its peak position
PK POS: Highest charted position record attained
RANK: Top 40 ranking

TOP 40 HITS
1955

PK DATE	PK WKS	PK POS	RANK	TITLE	ARTIST
7/09	8	1	1.	Rock Around The Clock	Bill Haley & His Comets
11/26	8	1	2.	Sixteen Tons	"Tennessee" Ernie Ford
10/08	6	1	③	Love Is A Many-Splendored Thing	Four Aces ✓
9/03	6	1	4.	The Yellow Rose Of Texas	Mitch Miller
10/29	4	1	⑤	Autumn Leaves	Roger Williams ✓
7/09	2	1	6.	Learnin' The Blues	Frank Sinatra
9/17	2	1	7.	Ain't That A Shame	Pat Boone
10/29	6	2	8.	Moments To Remember	The Four Lads
12/10	3	2	9.	I Hear You Knocking	Gale Storm
7/09	1	2	10.	A Blossom Fell	Nat "King" Cole
11/26	2	3	11.	The Shifting, Whispering Sands	Rusty Draper
10/08	1	3	12.	Seventeen	The Fontane Sisters
9/17	1	3	13.	The Yellow Rose Of Texas	Johnny Desmond
8/13	1	4	14.	Hard To Get	Gisele MacKenzie
12/31	1	4	15.	He	Al Hibbler
10/22	4	5	16.	The Shifting Whispering Sands (Parts 1 & 2)	Billy Vaughn
11/05	3	5	⑰	Only You (And You Alone)	The Platters ✓
11/26	3	5	18.	Love And Marriage	Frank Sinatra
10/15	1	5	19.	Tina Marie	Perry Como
7/23	1	5	20.	Something's Gotta Give	The McGuire Sisters
9/10	1	5	21.	Maybellene	Chuck Berry
9/24	1	5	22.	Wake The Town And Tell The People	Les Baxter
9/03	1	5	23.	Seventeen	Boyd Bennett & his Rockets
9/17	1	6	24.	The Longest Walk	Jaye P. Morgan
10/29	1	6	25.	Black Denim Trousers	The Cheers
11/05	1	6	26.	You Are My Love	Joni James
12/31	1	6	27.	Nuttin' For Christmas	Barry Gordon with Art Mooney
11/19	2	7	28.	At My Front Door (Crazy Little Mama)	Pat Boone
10/22	2	7	29.	The Bible Tells Me So	Don Cornell
8/27	2	7	30.	Hummingbird	Les Paul & Mary Ford
8/13	1	7	31.	It's A Sin To Tell A Lie	Somethin' Smith & The Redheads
12/31	1	7	㉜	White Christmas	Bing Crosby ✓
12/31	1	8	33.	Only You (And You Alone)	The Hilltoppers
7/16	1	8	34.	If I May	Nat "King" Cole & The Four Knights
7/16	1	9	35.	Something's Gotta Give	Sammy Davis, Jr.
8/27	1	9	36.	The House Of Blue Lights	Chuck Miller
12/17	1	9	37.	Cry Me A River	Julie London
12/31	1	9	38.	Burn That Candle	Bill Haley & His Comets
10/29	1	9	39.	Suddenly There's A Valley	Gogi Grant
7/09	3	10	40.	Sweet And Gentle	Alan Dale

Note The above ranking begins with the nation's first #1 rock hit "Rock Around The Clock" from the summer of 1955, and does not include the earlier hits from 1955.

TOP 40 HITS
1956

PK DATE	PK WKS	PK POS	RANK	TITLE	ARTIST
8/18	11	1	1.	Don't Be Cruel/Hound Dog	Elvis Presley
12/08	10	1	2.	Singing The Blues	Guy Mitchell
6/16	8	1	3.	The Wayward Wind	Gogi Grant
4/21	8	1	4.	Heartbreak Hotel	Elvis Presley
2/18	6	1	5.	Rock And Roll Waltz	Kay Starr
3/17	6	1	6.	The Poor People Of Paris	Les Baxter
1/07	6	1	7.	Memories Are Made Of This	Dean Martin
11/03	5	1	8.	Love Me Tender	Elvis Presley
8/04	5	1	9.	My Prayer	The Platters ✓
2/25	4	1	10.	Lisbon Antigua	Nelson Riddle
7/28	4	1	11.	I Almost Lost My Mind	Pat Boone
11/03	3	1	12.	The Green Door	Jim Lowe
6/02	3	1	13.	Moonglow and Theme From "Picnic"	Morris Stoloff
2/18	2	1	14.	The Great Pretender	The Platters ✓
5/05	1	1	15.	Hot Diggity (Dog Ziggity Boom)	Perry Como
7/28	1	1	16.	I Want You, I Need You, I Love You	Elvis Presley
3/17	4	2	17.	No, Not Much!	The Four Lads
5/19	4	2	18.	Blue Suede Shoes	Carl Perkins ✓
10/06	3	2	19.	Honky Tonk (Parts 1 & 2)	Bill Doggett
8/18	3	2	20.	Whatever Will Be, Will Be (Que Sera, Sera)	Doris Day
10/13	2	2	21.	Canadian Sunset	Hugo Winterhalter/Eddie Heywood
8/18	2	2	22.	Allegheny Moon	Patti Page
10/27	1	2	23.	Just Walking In The Rain	Johnnie Ray
6/16	1	2	24.	Ivory Tower	Cathy Carr
6/16	3	3	25.	Standing On The Corner	The Four Lads
7/14	2	3	26.	I'm In Love Again	Fats Domino
11/10	1	3	27.	True Love	Bing Crosby & Grace Kelly
8/25	1	3	28.	The Flying Saucer (Parts 1 & 2)	Buchanan & Goodman
7/07	4	4	29.	On The Street Where You Live	Vic Damone
5/19	3	4	30.	(You've Got) The Magic Touch	The Platters ✓
4/07	1	4	31.	I'll Be Home	Pat Boone
1/07	1	4	32.	Band Of Gold	Don Cherry
10/06	1	4	33.	Tonight You Belong To Me	Patience & Prudence
6/02	1	4	34.	Moonglow And Theme From "Picnic"	George Cates
7/21	1	4	35.	More	Perry Como ✓
5/12	2	5	36.	A Tear Fell	Teresa Brewer
7/14	2	5	37.	Born To Be With You	The Chordettes
10/20	1	5	38.	Friendly Persuasion (Thee I Love)	Pat Boone
1/14	1	5	39.	Memories Are Made Of This	Gale Storm
2/11	4	6	40.	See You Later, Alligator	Bill Haley & His Comets

TOP 40 HITS
1957

PK DATE	PK WKS	PK POS	RANK	TITLE	ARTIST
4/13	9	1	1.	All Shook Up	Elvis Presley
6/03	7	1	2.	Love Letters In The Sand	Pat Boone
10/21	7	1	3.	Jailhouse Rock	Elvis Presley
7/08	7	1	4.	(Let Me Be Your) Teddy Bear	Elvis Presley
12/16	6	1	5.	April Love	Pat Boone
2/16	6	1	6.	Young Love	Tab Hunter
8/19	5	1	7.	Tammy	Debbie Reynolds
9/23	4	1	8.	Honeycomb	Jimmie Rodgers
10/14	4	1	9.	Wake Up Little Susie	The Everly Brothers
12/02	3	1	10.	You Send Me	Sam Cooke
3/30	3	1	11.	Butterfly	Andy Williams
2/09	3	1	12.	Too Much	Elvis Presley
4/06	2	1	13.	Round And Round	Perry Como
4/13	2	1	14.	Butterfly	Charlie Gracie
10/21	1	1	15.	Chances Are	Johnny Mathis
2/09	1	1	16.	Don't Forbid Me	Pat Boone
2/09	1	1	17.	Young Love	Sonny James
9/09	1	1	18.	Diana	Paul Anka ✓
3/30	1	1	19.	Party Doll	Buddy Knox/The Rhythm Orchids
9/23	1	1	20.	That'll Be The Day	The Crickets
4/06	8	2	21.	Little Darlin'	The Diamonds
6/17	4	2	22.	So Rare	Jimmy Dorsey
6/17	4	2	23.	Bye Bye Love	The Everly Brothers
1/19	3	2	24.	Blueberry Hill	Fats Domino ✓
1/05	2	2	25.	Love Me	Elvis Presley
3/16	2	2	26.	Teen-Age Crush	Tommy Sands
6/03	1	2	27.	A White Sport Coat (And A Pink Carnation)	Marty Robbins
12/16	1	2	28.	Raunchy	Bill Justis
6/10	1	2	29.	A Teenager's Romance	Ricky Nelson
8/05	4	3	30.	I'm Gonna Sit Right Down And Write Myself A Letter	Billy Williams
12/16	3	3	31.	Kisses Sweeter Than Wine	Jimmie Rodgers
12/30	3	3	32.	Peggy Sue	Buddy Holly
5/13	3	3	33.	School Day	Chuck Berry ✓
9/09	2	3	34.	Whole Lot Of Shakin' Going On	Jerry Lee Lewis
11/04	2	3	35.	Silhouettes	The Rays ✓
7/29	1	3	36.	Searchin'	The Coasters
7/29	1	3	37.	Old Cape Cod	Patti Page
1/19	1	3	38.	Moonlight Gambler	Frankie Laine
1/12	1	3	39.	Hey! Jealous Lover	Frank Sinatra
4/06	1	3	40.	Marianne	The Hilltoppers

TOP 40 HITS
1958

PK DATE	PK WKS	PK POS	RANK	TITLE	ARTIST
1/06	7	1	1.	At The Hop	Danny & The Juniors
9/29	6	1	2.	It's All In The Game	Tommy Edwards
6/09	6	1	3.	The Purple People Eater	Sheb Wooley
5/12	5	1	4.	All I Have To Do Is Dream	The Everly Brothers
3/17	5	1	5.	Tequila	The Champs
2/10	5	1	6.	Don't	Elvis Presley
8/18	5	1	7.	Nel Blu Dipinto Di Blu (Volare)	Domenico Modugno
2/17	4	1	8.	Sugartime	The McGuire Sisters
4/14	4	1	9.	He's Got The Whole World (In His Hands)	Laurie London
12/22	4	1	10.	The Chipmunk Song	The Chipmunks/David Seville
4/28	3	1	11.	Witch Doctor	David Seville
12/01	3	1	12.	To Know Him, Is To Love Him	The Teddy Bears
8/04	2	1	13.	Poor Little Fool	Ricky Nelson
11/10	2	1	14.	It's Only Make Believe	Conway Twitty
2/24	2	1	15.	Get A Job	The Silhouettes
7/21	2	1	16.	Hard Headed Woman	Elvis Presley
7/28	1	1	17.	Patricia	Perez Prado
11/17	1	1	18.	Tom Dooley	The Kingston Trio
3/24	1	1	19.	Catch A Falling Star	Perry Como
4/21	1	1	20.	Twilight Time	The Platters
8/25	1	1	21.	Little Star	The Elegants
8/25	1	1	22.	Bird Dog	The Everly Brothers
7/21	1	1	23.	Yakety Yak	The Coasters
1/06	4	2	24.	Great Balls Of Fire	Jerry Lee Lewis
3/10	3	2	25.	26 Miles (Santa Catalina)	The Four Preps
1/13	3	2	26.	Stood Up	Ricky Nelson
3/17	3	2	27.	Sweet Little Sixteen	Chuck Berry
10/13	2	2	28.	Rock-in Robin	Bobby Day
3/31	2	2	29.	Lollipop	The Chordettes
1/06	1	2	30.	All The Way	Frank Sinatra
4/28	1	2	31.	Wear My Ring Around Your Neck	Elvis Presley
12/15	1	2	32.	Problems	The Everly Brothers
6/16	3	3	33.	Secretly	Jimmie Rodgers
10/20	3	3	34.	Topsy II	Cozy Cole
6/09	2	3	35.	Big Man	The Four Preps
2/10	2	3	36.	Short Shorts	Royal Teens
8/18	1	3	37.	My True Love	Jack Scott
3/24	1	3	38.	Are You Sincere	Andy Williams
8/04	1	3	39.	Splish Splash	Bobby Darin
3/10	5	4	40.	A Wonderful Time Up There	Pat Boone

TOP 40 HITS
1959

PK DATE	PK WKS	PK POS	RANK	TITLE	ARTIST
10/05	9	1	1.	Mack The Knife	Bobby Darin
6/01	6	1	2.	The Battle Of New Orleans	Johnny Horton
3/09	5	1	3.	Venus	Frankie Avalon ✓
2/09	4	1	4.	Stagger Lee	Lloyd Price
8/24	4	1	5.	The Three Bells	The Browns
7/13	4	1	6.	Lonely Boy	Paul Anka ✓
4/13	4	1	7.	Come Softly To Me	Fleetwoods
1/19	3	1	8.	Smoke Gets In Your Eyes	The Platters ✓
12/14	2	1	9.	Heartaches By The Number	Guy Mitchell
9/21	2	1	10.	Sleep Walk	Santo & Johnny ✓
5/18	2	1	11.	Kansas City	Wilbert Harrison
8/10	2	1	12.	A Big Hunk O' Love	Elvis Presley
11/16	1	1	13.	Mr. Blue	The Fleetwoods
12/28	1	1	14.	Why	Frankie Avalon
5/11	1	1	15.	The Happy Organ	Dave 'Baby' Cortez
10/05	3	2	16.	Put Your Head On My Shoulder	Paul Anka ✓
6/15	3	2	17.	Personality	Lloyd Price
3/09	3	2	18.	Charlie Brown	The Coasters
2/23	2	2	19.	Donna	Ritchie Valens
2/09	2	2	20.	16 Candles	The Crests ✓
1/19	2	2	21.	My Happiness	Connie Francis
5/11	2	2	22.	Sorry (I Ran All the Way Home)	The Impalas
8/24	2	2	23.	Sea Of Love	Phil Phillips ✓
6/08	1	2	24.	Dream Lover	Bobby Darin ✓
11/30	1	2	25.	Don't You Know	Della Reese
8/17	1	2	26.	There Goes My Baby	The Drifters ✓
2/02	1	2	27.	The All American Boy	Bill Parsons (Bobby Bare)
4/27	1	2	28.	(Now And Then There's) A Fool Such As I	Elvis Presley
8/03	3	3	29.	My Heart Is An Open Book	Carl Dobkins, Jr.
4/13	2	3	30.	Pink Shoe Laces	Dodie Stevens ✓
12/28	2	3	31.	The Big Hurt	Miss Toni Fisher
9/14	2	3	32.	I'm Gonna Get Married	Lloyd Price
7/20	2	3	33.	Tiger	Fabian ✓
3/16	2	3	34.	Alvin's Harmonica	The Chipmunks
4/06	1	3	35.	It's Just A Matter Of Time	Brook Benton
8/24	1	3	36.	Lavender-Blue	Sammy Turner
9/21	3	4	37.	('Til) I Kissed You	The Everly Brothers
7/13	3	4	38.	Waterloo	Stonewall Jackson
10/19	2	4	39.	Teen Beat	Sandy Nelson
6/01	2	4	40.	Quiet Village	Martin Denny

TOP 40 HITS
1960

PK DATE	PK WKS	PK POS	RANK	TITLE	ARTIST
2/22	9	1	①.	The Theme From "A Summer Place"	Percy Faith
11/28	6	1	2.	Are You Lonesome To-night?	Elvis Presley
8/15	5	1	3.	It's Now Or Never.................................	Elvis Presley
5/23	5	1	④.	Cathy's Clown...............................	The Everly Brothers
4/25	4	1	5.	Stuck On You......................................	Elvis Presley
7/18	3	1	6.	I'm Sorry	Brenda Lee
1/18	3	1	7.	Running Bear	Johnny Preston
10/17	3	1	⑧.	Save The Last Dance For Me	The Drifters
2/08	2	1	9.	Teen Angel......................................	Mark Dinning
9/26	2	1	10.	My Heart Has A Mind Of Its Own	Connie Francis
1/04	2	1	11.	El Paso...	Marty Robbins
6/27	2	1	12.	Everybody's Somebody's Fool	Connie Francis
9/19	1	1	13.	The Twist .... re-entered at #1 in 1962	Chubby Checker
8/08	1	1	14.	Itsy Bitsy Teenie Weenie Yellow Polkadot Bikini	Brian Hyland
7/11	1	1	15.	Alley-Oop..	Hollywood Argyles
10/10	1	1	16.	Mr. Custer.......................................	Larry Verne
10/24	1	1	17.	I Want To Be Wanted	Brenda Lee
11/21	1	1	⑱	Stay	Maurice Williams & The Zodiacs
11/14	1	1	19.	Georgia On My Mind..............................	Ray Charles
11/28	4	2	20.	Last Date..	Floyd Cramer
4/18	4	2	21.	Greenfields.......................................	The Brothers Four
3/07	3	2	22.	He'll Have To Go	Jim Reeves
10/03	2	2	23.	Chain Gang.......................................	Sam Cooke
4/04	2	2	㉔	Puppy Love	Paul Anka
2/29	1	2	25.	Handy Man	Jimmy Jones
8/29	1	2	㉖	Walk--Don't Run.................................	The Ventures
7/25	1	2	27.	Only The Lonely (Know How I Feel)	Roy Orbison
3/28	1	2	28.	Wild One	Bobby Rydell
11/14	1	2	29.	Poetry In Motion	Johnny Tillotson
5/23	3	3	30.	Good Timin'.....................................	Jimmy Jones
6/13	2	3	31.	Burning Bridges.................................	Jack Scott
12/12	1	3	32.	A Thousand Stars................................	Kathy Young with The Innocents
5/02	1	3	33.	Sixteen Reasons	Connie Stevens
4/25	1	3	34.	Sink The Bismarck	Johnny Horton
1/11	1	3	35.	Way Down Yonder In New Orleans.............	Freddie Cannon
2/08	1	3	36.	Where Or When.................................	Dion & The Belmonts
11/14	1	3	37.	You Talk Too Much	Joe Jones
5/09	2	4	38.	Night..	Jackie Wilson
5/30	2	4	39.	He'll Have To Stay	Jeanne Black
7/04	2	4	40.	Because They're Young...........................	Duane Eddy & The Rebels

TOP 40 HITS
1961

PK DATE	PK WKS	PK POS	RANK	TITLE	ARTIST
7/10	7	1	1.	Tossin' And Turnin'	Bobby Lewis
11/06	5	1	2.	Big Bad John	Jimmy Dean
4/24	4	1	3.	Runaway	Del Shannon
1/09	3	1	4.	Wonderland By Night	Bert Kaempfert
2/27	3	1	5.	Pony Time	Chubby Checker
12/18	3	1	6.	The Lion Sleeps Tonight	The Tokens
4/03	3	1	7.	Blue Moon	The Marcels ✓
9/18	3	1	8.	Take Good Care Of My Baby	Bobby Vee
2/13	2	1	9.	Calcutta	Lawrence Welk
10/23	2	1	10.	Runaround Sue	Dion
9/04	2	1	11.	Michael	The Highwaymen
5/29	2	1	12.	Travelin' Man	Ricky Nelson
6/26	2	1	13.	Quarter To Three	U.S. Bonds
10/09	2	1	14.	Hit The Road Jack	Ray Charles
3/20	2	1	15.	Surrender	Elvis Presley
1/30	2	1	16.	Will You Love Me Tomorrow	The Shirelles
5/22	1	1	17.	Mother-In-Law	Ernie K-Doe ✓
12/11	1	1	18.	Please Mr. Postman	The Marvelettes
8/28	1	1	19.	Wooden Heart	Joe Dowell
6/19	1	1	20.	Moody River	Pat Boone
6/05	1	1	21.	Running Scared	Roy Orbison
7/10	3	2	22.	The Boll Weevil Song	Brook Benton
7/31	3	2	23.	I Like It Like That, Part 1	Chris Kenner
10/23	2	2	24.	Bristol Stomp	The Dovells
4/03	2	2	25.	Apache	Jorgen Ingmann & His Guitar
9/25	2	2	26.	The Mountain's High	Dick & DeeDee
1/23	1	2	27.	Exodus	Ferrante & Teicher
6/26	1	2	28.	Raindrops	Dee Clark ✓
2/20	1	2	29.	Shop Around	The Miracles
12/25	1	2	30.	Run To Him	Bobby Vee
10/09	1	2	31.	Crying	Roy Orbison
5/29	1	2	32.	Daddy's Home	Shep & The Limelites
3/27	2	3	33.	Dedicated To The One I Love	The Shirelles
5/08	2	3	34.	A Hundred Pounds Of Clay	Gene McDaniels ✓
12/04	2	3	35.	Goodbye Cruel World	James Darren
3/06	2	3	36.	Wheels	The String-A-Longs
8/07	2	3	37.	Last Night	Mar-Keys
11/13	2	3	38.	Fool #1	Brenda Lee
9/11	2	3	39.	My True Story	The Jive Five
3/20	1	3	40.	Don't Worry	Marty Robbins

TOP 40 HITS
1962

PK DATE	PK WKS	PK POS	RANK	TITLE	ARTIST
6/02	5	1	1.	I Can't Stop Loving You	Ray Charles
11/17	5	1	2.	Big Girls Don't Cry	The 4 Seasons
9/15	5	1	3.	Sherry	The 4 Seasons
7/14	4	1	4.	Roses Are Red (My Love)	Bobby Vinton
1/27	3	1	5.	Peppermint Twist - Part I	Joey Dee & the Starliters
12/22	3	1	6.	Telstar	The Tornadoes
5/05	3	1	7.	Soldier Boy	The Shirelles
3/10	3	1	8.	Hey! Baby	Bruce Channel
2/17	3	1	9.	Duke Of Earl	Gene Chandler
1/13	2	1	10.	The Twist	Chubby Checker
				re-entry of 1960 hit (POS 1)	
4/07	2	1	11.	Johnny Angel	Shelley Fabares
11/03	2	1	12.	He's A Rebel	The Crystals
8/11	2	1	13.	Breaking Up Is Hard To Do	Neil Sedaka
10/20	2	1	14.	Monster Mash	Bobby "Boris" Pickett & The Crypt-Kickers
4/21	2	1	15.	Good Luck Charm	Elvis Presley
9/01	2	1	16.	Sheila	Tommy Roe
5/26	1	1	17.	Stranger On The Shore	Mr. Acker Bilk
7/07	1	1	18.	The Stripper	David Rose
8/25	1	1	19.	The Loco-Motion	Little Eva
3/31	1	1	20.	Don't Break The Heart That Loves You	Connie Francis
11/17	5	2	21.	Return To Sender	Elvis Presley
12/22	2	2	22.	Limbo Rock	Chubby Checker
5/05	2	2	23.	Mashed Potato Time	Dee Dee Sharp
9/22	2	2	24.	Ramblin' Rose	Nat King Cole
7/21	2	2	25.	The Wah Watusi	The Orlons
2/03	1	2	26.	Can't Help Falling In Love	Elvis Presley
2/24	1	2	27.	The Wanderer	Dion
3/17	1	2	28.	Midnight In Moscow	Kenny Ball & his Jazzmen
9/08	1	2	29.	You Don't Know Me	Ray Charles
11/03	1	2	30.	Only Love Can Break A Heart	Gene Pitney
12/01	4	3	31.	Bobby's Girl	Marcie Blane
10/20	3	3	32.	Do You Love Me	The Contours
11/10	2	3	33.	All Alone Am I	Brenda Lee
6/23	2	3	34.	Palisades Park	Freddy Cannon
7/28	2	3	35.	Sealed With A Kiss	Brian Hyland
4/14	1	3	36.	Slow Twistin'	Chubby Checker
2/24	1	3	37.	Norman	Sue Thompson
9/29	1	3	38.	Green Onions	Booker T. & The MG's
6/16	1	3	39.	It Keeps Right On A-Hurtin'	Johnny Tillotson
1/27	1	3	40.	I Know (You Don't Love Me No More)	Barbara George

FREDDIE'S DEAD

A POWERFUL SINGLE FROM A POWERFUL ARTIST.

CURTIS MAYFIELD

FROM THE ALBUM SUPERFLY
CURTIS' ORIGINAL SOUNDTRACK FROM THE WARNER BROTHERS' MOVIE
FREDDIE'S DEAD, THE SINGLE CR 1975
SUPERFLY, THE ALBUM CRS 8014-ST

CURTOM RECORDS

FROM THE BUDDAH GROUP

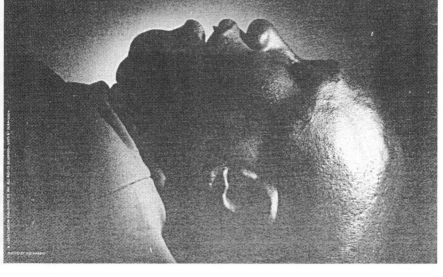

TOP 40 HITS
1963

PK DATE	PK WKS	PK POS	RANK	TITLE	ARTIST
10/12	5	1	1.	Sugar Shack	Jimmy Gilmer & The Fireballs
3/30	4	1	2.	He's So Fine	The Chiffons
12/07	4	1	3.	Dominique	The Singing Nun
2/09	3	1	4.	Hey Paula	Paul & Paula
8/31	3	1	5.	My Boyfriend's Back	The Angels
9/21	3	1	6.	Blue Velvet	Bobby Vinton ✓
6/15	3	1	7.	Sukiyaki	Kyu Sakamoto
4/27	3	1	8.	I Will Follow Him	Little Peggy March
8/10	3	1	9.	Fingertips - Pt 2	Little Stevie Wonder
3/02	3	1	10.	Walk Like A Man	The 4 Seasons
1/12	2	1	11.	Go Away Little Girl	Steve Lawrence
11/23	2	1	12.	I'm Leaving It Up To You	Dale & Grace
7/20	2	1	13.	Surf City	Jan & Dean
6/01	2	1	14.	It's My Party	Lesley Gore
1/26	2	1	15.	Walk Right In	The Rooftop Singers
7/06	2	1	16.	Easier Said Than Done	The Essex
5/18	2	1	17.	If You Wanna Be Happy	Jimmy Soul
8/03	1	1	18.	So Much In Love	The Tymes
11/16	1	1	19.	Deep Purple	Nino Tempo & April Stevens
3/23	1	1	20.	Our Day Will Come	Ruby & The Romantics
12/14	6	2	21.	Louie Louie	The Kingsmen
4/13	4	2	22.	Can't Get Used To Losing You	Andy Williams
2/23	3	2	23.	Ruby Baby	Dion
10/12	3	2	24.	Be My Baby	The Ronettes ✓
8/24	3	2	25.	Hello Mudduh, Hello Fadduh! (A Letter From Camp)	Allan Sherman
9/28	2	2	26.	Sally, Go 'Round The Roses	The Jaynetts
8/17	1	2	27.	Blowin' In The Wind	Peter, Paul & Mary ✓
11/23	1	2	28.	Washington Square	The Village Stompers
8/10	1	2	29.	Wipe Out	The Surfaris
3/23	1	2	30.	The End Of The World	Skeeter Davis
5/11	1	2	31.	Puff The Magic Dragon	Peter, Paul & Mary ✓
9/07	3	3	32.	If I Had A Hammer	Trini Lopez
3/16	2	3	33.	You're The Reason I'm Living	Bobby Darin
2/02	2	3	34.	The Night Has A Thousand Eyes	Bobby Vee
12/07	2	3	35.	Everybody	Tommy Roe
8/10	2	3	36.	(You're the) Devil In Disguise	Elvis Presley
6/22	2	3	37.	Hello Stranger	Barbara Lewis
3/09	1	3	38.	Rhythm Of The Rain	The Cascades
5/25	1	3	39.	Surfin' U.S.A.	Beach Boys
6/01	1	3	40.	I Love You Because	Al Martino

TOP 40 HITS
1964

PK DATE	PK WKS	PK POS	RANK	TITLE	ARTIST
2/01	7	1	1.	I Want To Hold Your Hand	The Beatles
4/04	5	1	2.	Can't Buy Me Love	The Beatles
1/04	4	1	3.	There! I've Said It Again	Bobby Vinton
10/31	4	1	4.	Baby Love	The Supremes
9/26	3	1	5.	Oh, Pretty Woman	Roy Orbison
9/05	3	1	6.	The House Of The Rising Sun	The Animals
6/06	3	1	7.	Chapel Of Love	The Dixie Cups
12/26	3	1	8.	I Feel Fine	The Beatles
3/21	2	1	9.	She Loves You	The Beatles
7/04	2	1	10.	I Get Around	The Beach Boys
12/19	2	1	11.	Come See About Me	The Supremes
8/22	2	1	12.	Where Did Our Love Go	The Supremes
10/17	2	1	13.	Do Wah Diddy Diddy	Manfred Mann
5/16	2	1	14.	My Guy	Mary Wells
8/01	2	1	15.	A Hard Day's Night	The Beatles
7/18	2	1	16.	Rag Doll	The 4 Seasons
5/09	1	1	17.	Hello, Dolly!	Louis Armstrong
12/12	1	1	18.	Mr. Lonely	Bobby Vinton
8/15	1	1	19.	Everybody Loves Somebody	Dean Martin
6/27	1	1	20.	A World Without Love	Peter & Gordon
12/05	1	1	21.	Ringo	Lorne Greene
5/30	1	1	22.	Love Me Do	The Beatles
11/28	1	1	23.	Leader Of The Pack	The Shangri-Las
4/04	4	2	24.	Twist And Shout	The Beatles
2/01	3	2	25.	You Don't Own Me	Lesley Gore
10/17	2	2	26.	Dancing In The Street	Martha & The Vandellas
9/19	2	2	27.	Bread And Butter	The Newbeats
7/11	2	2	28.	Memphis	Johnny Rivers
11/07	1	2	29.	Last Kiss	J. Frank Wilson & The Cavaliers
12/12	1	2	30.	She's Not There	The Zombies
7/04	1	2	31.	My Boy Lollipop	Millie Small
5/09	1	2	32.	Do You Want To Know A Secret	The Beatles
2/22	3	3	33.	Dawn (Go Away)	The Four Seasons
4/11	2	3	34.	Suspicion	Terry Stafford
3/14	2	3	35.	Please Please Me	The Beatles
1/11	2	3	36.	Popsicles And Icicles	The Murmaids
2/01	2	3	37.	Out Of Limits	The Marketts
11/21	2	3	38.	Come A Little Bit Closer	Jay & The Americans
6/13	1	3	39.	Love Me With All Your Heart (Cuando Calienta El Sol)	The Ray Charles Singers
8/01	1	3	40.	The Little Old Lady (From Pasadena)	Jan & Dean

TOP 40 HITS
1965

PK DATE	PK WKS	PK POS	RANK	TITLE	ARTIST
7/10	4	1	1.	(I Can't Get No) Satisfaction	The Rolling Stones
10/09	4	1	2.	Yesterday	The Beatles
12/04	3	1	3.	Turn! Turn! Turn! (To Everything There Is A Season)	The Byrds
5/01	3	1	4.	Mrs. Brown You've Got A Lovely Daughter	Herman's Hermits
8/14	3	1	5.	I Got You Babe	Sonny & Cher
9/04	3	1	6.	Help!	The Beatles
6/19	2	1	7.	I Can't Help Myself	Four Tops
2/06	2	1	8.	You've Lost That Lovin' Feelin'	The Righteous Brothers
1/23	2	1	9.	Downtown	Petula Clark
2/20	2	1	10.	This Diamond Ring	Gary Lewis & The Playboys
3/27	2	1	11.	Stop! In The Name Of Love	The Supremes
5/29	2	1	12.	Help Me, Rhonda	The Beach Boys
11/06	2	1	13.	Get Off Of My Cloud	The Rolling Stones
11/20	2	1	14.	I Hear A Symphony	The Supremes
4/10	2	1	15.	I'm Telling You Now	Freddie & The Dreamers
3/13	2	1	16.	Eight Days A Week	The Beatles
3/06	1	1	17.	My Girl	The Temptations
10/02	1	1	18.	Hang On Sloopy	The McCoys
6/26	1	1	19.	Mr. Tambourine Man	The Byrds
9/25	1	1	20.	Eve Of Destruction	Barry McGuire
12/25	1	1	21.	Over And Over	The Dave Clark Five
5/22	1	1	22.	Ticket To Ride	The Beatles
8/07	1	1	23.	I'm Henry VIII, I Am	Herman's Hermits
4/24	1	1	24.	Game Of Love	Wayne Fontana/The Mindbenders
6/12	1	1	25.	Back In My Arms Again	The Supremes
10/30	3	2	26.	A Lover's Concerto	The Toys
6/05	2	2	27.	Wooly Bully	Sam The Sham & The Pharoahs
3/27	2	2	28.	Can't You Hear My Heartbeat	Herman's Hermits
9/04	2	2	29.	Like A Rolling Stone	Bob Dylan
10/16	2	2	30.	Treat Her Right	Roy Head & The Traits
5/08	2	2	31.	Count Me In	Gary Lewis & The Playboys
11/20	1	2	32.	1-2-3	Len Barry
8/21	1	2	33.	Save Your Heart For Me	Gary Lewis & The Playboys
12/18	3	3	34.	I Got You (I Feel Good)	James Brown
3/20	2	3	35.	The Birds And The Bees	Jewel Akens
1/16	2	3	36.	Love Potion Number Nine	The Searchers
1/30	2	3	37.	The Name Game	Shirley Ellis
7/31	2	3	38.	What's New Pussycat?	Tom Jones
8/28	2	3	39.	California Girls	The Beach Boys
12/11	1	3	40.	Let's Hang On!	The 4 Seasons

TOP 40 HITS
1966

PK DATE	PK WKS	PK POS	RANK	TITLE	ARTIST
12/31	7	1	1.	I'm A Believer	The Monkees
3/05	5	1	2.	The Ballad Of The Green Berets	SSgt Barry Sadler
12/03	3	1	(3.)	Winchester Cathedral	The New Vaudeville Band
4/09	3	1	4.	(You're My) Soul And Inspiration	The Righteous Brothers
5/07	3	1	(5.)	Monday, Monday	The Mama's & The Papa's
1/08	3	1	6.	We Can Work It Out	The Beatles
8/13	3	1	7.	Summer In The City	The Lovin' Spoonful
9/24	3	1	8.	Cherish	The Association
9/10	2	1	9.	You Can't Hurry Love	The Supremes
7/30	2	1	10.	Wild Thing	The Troggs
10/15	2	1	11.	Reach Out I'll Be There	Four Tops
6/11	2	1	12.	Paint It, Black	The Rolling Stones
5/28	2	1	13.	When A Man Loves A Woman	Percy Sledge
11/19	2	1	14.	You Keep Me Hangin' On	The Supremes
7/16	2	1	15.	Hanky Panky	Tommy James & The Shondells
2/05	2	1	16.	My Love	Petula Clark
1/01	2	1	(17.)	The Sounds Of Silence	Simon & Garfunkel
6/25	2	1	18.	Paperback Writer	The Beatles
10/29	1	1	19.	96 Tears	? & The Mysterians
11/05	1	1	20.	Last Train To Clarksville	The Monkees
11/12	1	1	21.	Poor Side Of Town	Johnny Rivers
2/26	1	1	22.	These Boots Are Made For Walkin'	Nancy Sinatra
12/10	1	1	23.	Good Vibrations	The Beach Boys
4/30	1	1	24.	Good Lovin'	The Young Rascals
7/02	1	1	(25.)	Strangers In The Night	Frank Sinatra
9/03	1	1	26.	Sunshine Superman	Donovan
2/19	1	1	27.	Lightnin' Strikes	Lou Christie
12/31	4	2	28.	Snoopy Vs. The Red Baron	The Royal Guardsmen
12/10	3	2	29.	Mellow Yellow	Donovan
3/19	3	2	30.	19th Nervous Breakdown	The Rolling Stones
8/06	2	2	31.	Lil' Red Riding Hood	Sam The Sham & The Pharoahs
4/09	2	2	32.	Daydream	The Lovin' Spoonful
8/20	2	2	33.	Sunny	Bobby Hebb
6/11	2	2	34.	Did You Ever Have To Make Up Your Mind?	The Lovin' Spoonful
5/28	2	2	35.	A Groovy Kind Of Love	The Mindbenders
1/29	2	2	36.	Barbara Ann	The Beach Boys
7/09	1	2	37.	Red Rubber Ball	The Cyrkle
4/23	1	2	38.	Bang Bang (My Baby Shot Me Down)	Cher
9/17	1	2	39.	Yellow Submarine	The Beatles
5/21	1	2	40.	Rainy Day Women #12 & 35	Bob Dylan

TOP 40 HITS
1967

PK DATE	PK WKS	PK POS	RANK	TITLE	ARTIST
10/21	5	1	1.	To Sir With Love	Lulu
12/02	4	1	2.	Daydream Believer	The Monkees
7/01	4	1	3.	Windy	The Association
8/26	4	1	4.	Ode To Billie Joe	Bobbie Gentry
4/15	4	1	5.	Somethin' Stupid	Nancy Sinatra & Frank Sinatra
5/20	4	1	6.	Groovin'	The Young Rascals
9/23	4	1	7.	The Letter	The Box Tops
7/29	3	1	8.	Light My Fire	The Doors
3/25	3	1	9.	Happy Together	The Turtles
12/30	3	1	10.	Hello Goodbye	The Beatles
6/03	2	1	11.	Respect	Aretha Franklin
2/18	2	1	(12.)	Kind Of A Drag	The Buckinghams
11/25	1	1	13.	Incense And Peppermints	Strawberry Alarm Clock
3/11	1	1	14.	Love Is Here And Now You're Gone	The Supremes
3/04	1	1	15.	Ruby Tuesday	The Rolling Stones
8/19	1	1	16.	All You Need Is Love	The Beatles
5/13	1	1	17.	The Happening	The Supremes
3/18	1	1	18.	Penny Lane	The Beatles
12/16	3	2	19.	I Heard It Through The Grapevine	Gladys Knight & The Pips
11/04	3	2	20.	Soul Man	Sam & Dave
3/25	3	2	21.	Dedicated To The One I Love	The Mamas & The Papas
7/08	2	2	22.	Little Bit O' Soul	The Music Explosion
12/02	2	2	23.	The Rain, The Park & Other Things	The Cowsills
2/04	2	2	(24.)	Georgy Girl	The Seekers
10/07	2	2	25.	Never My Love	The Association
7/29	2	2	26.	I Was Made To Love Her	Stevie Wonder
9/09	2	2	27.	Reflections	Diana Ross & The Supremes
7/22	1	2	28.	Can't Take My Eyes Off You	Frankie Valli
1/28	1	2	29.	Tell It Like It Is	Aaron Neville
5/13	1	2	30.	Sweet Soul Music	Arthur Conley
4/29	1	2	31.	A Little Bit Me, A Little Bit You	The Monkees
9/09	3	3	32.	Come Back When You Grow Up	Bobby Vee
5/27	3	3	33.	I Got Rhythm	The Happenings
11/04	2	3	34.	It Must Be Him	Vikki Carr
8/19	2	3	35.	Pleasant Valley Sunday	The Monkees
3/11	2	3	36.	Baby I Need Your Lovin'	Johnny Rivers
6/17	2	3	37.	She'd Rather Be With Me	The Turtles
4/15	1	3	38.	This Is My Song	Petula Clark
5/27	4	4	39.	Release Me (And Let Me Love Again)	Engelbert Humperdinck
7/01	4	4	(40.)	San Francisco (Be Sure To Wear Flowers In Your Hair)	Scott McKenzie

TOP 40 HITS
1968

PK DATE	PK WKS	PK POS	RANK	TITLE	ARTIST
9/28	9	1	1.	Hey Jude	The Beatles
12/14	7	1	2.	I Heard It Through The Grapevine	Marvin Gaye
2/10	5	1	3.	Love Is Blue	Paul Mauriat
4/13	5	1	4.	Honey	Bobby Goldsboro
8/17	5	1	5.	People Got To Be Free	The Rascals
3/16	4	1	6.	(Sittin' On) The Dock Of The Bay	Otis Redding
6/22	4	1	7.	This Guy's In Love With You	Herb Alpert
6/01	3	1	8.	Mrs. Robinson	Simon & Garfunkel
11/30	2	1	9.	Love Child	Diana Ross & The Supremes
5/18	2	1	10.	Tighten Up	Archie Bell & The Drells
8/03	2	1	11.	Hello, I Love You	The Doors
1/20	2	1	12.	Judy In Disguise (With Glasses)	John Fred & His Playboy Band
7/20	2	1	13.	Grazing In The Grass	Hugh Masekela
9/21	1	1	14.	Harper Valley P.T.A.	Jeannie C. Riley
2/03	1	1	15.	Green Tambourine	The Lemon Pipers
2/24	4	2	16.	(Theme From) Valley Of The Dolls	Dionne Warwick
4/06	3	2	(17.)	Young Girl	Union Gap feat. Gary Puckett ✓
11/02	3	2	18.	Those Were The Days	Mary Hopkin
6/29	3	2	19.	The Horse	Cliff Nobles & Co.
8/24	3	2	20.	Born To Be Wild	Steppenwolf
12/28	2	2	21.	For Once In My Life	Stevie Wonder
1/20	2	2	22.	Chain Of Fools	Aretha Franklin
4/27	2	2	23.	Cry Like A Baby	The Box Tops
8/03	2	2	24.	Classical Gas	Mason Williams
7/20	2	2	(25.)	Lady Willpower	Gary Puckett & The Union Gap ✓
10/26	1	2	26.	Little Green Apples	O.C. Smith
6/01	1	2	27.	The Good, The Bad And The Ugly	Hugo Montenegro
10/19	1	2	28.	Fire	The Crazy World Of Arthur Brown
6/22	1	2	29.	MacArthur Park	Richard Harris
7/27	3	3	30.	Stoned Soul Picnic	The 5th Dimension
2/10	3	3	(31.)	Spooky	Classics IV ✓
7/06	3	3	32.	Jumpin' Jack Flash	The Rolling Stones
8/31	3	3	33.	Light My Fire	Jose Feliciano
5/25	2	3	34.	A Beautiful Morning	The Rascals
3/30	2	3	35.	Valleri	The Monkees
11/30	1	3	36.	Magic Carpet Ride	Steppenwolf
6/15	1	3	37.	Mony Mony	Tommy James & The Shondells
3/09	4	4	38.	Simon Says	1910 Fruitgum Co.
1/13	3	4	(39.)	Woman, Woman	Union Gap feat. Gary Puckett ✓
2/17	3	4	40.	I Wish It Would Rain	The Temptations

TOP 40 HITS
1969

PK DATE	PK WKS	PK POS	RANK	TITLE	ARTIST
4/12	6	1	1.	Aquarius/Let The Sunshine In	The 5th Dimension
7/12	6	1	2.	In The Year 2525 (Exordium & Terminus)	Zager & Evans
5/24	5	1	3.	Get Back	The Beatles with Billy Preston
9/20	4	1	4.	Sugar, Sugar	The Archies
8/23	4	1	5.	Honky Tonk Women	The Rolling Stones
2/15	4	1	6.	Everyday People	Sly & The Family Stone
3/15	4	1	7.	Dizzy	Tommy Roe
11/08	3	1	8.	Wedding Bell Blues	The 5th Dimension
10/18	2	1	9.	I Can't Get Next To You	The Temptations
2/01	2	1	10.	Crimson And Clover	Tommy James & The Shondells
12/06	2	1	11.	Na Na Hey Hey Kiss Him Goodbye	Steam
6/28	2	1	12.	Love Theme From Romeo & Juliet	Henry Mancini
12/20	1	1	13.	Leaving On A Jet Plane	Peter, Paul & Mary
11/29	1	1	14.	Come Together	The Beatles
12/27	1	1	15.	Someday We'll Be Together	Diana Ross & The Supremes
11/01	1	1	16.	Suspicious Minds	Elvis Presley
7/26	3	2	17.	Crystal Blue Persuasion	Tommy James & The Shondells
3/08	3	2	18.	Proud Mary	Creedence Clearwater Revival
7/05	3	2	19.	Spinning Wheel	Blood, Sweat & Tears
8/23	3	2	20.	A Boy Named Sue	Johnny Cash
4/12	3	2	21.	You've Made Me So Very Happy	Blood, Sweat & Tears
5/10	2	2	22.	Hair	The Cowsills
1/11	2	2	23.	I'm Gonna Make You Love Me	Supremes & Temptations
10/18	2	2	24.	Hot Fun In The Summertime	Sly & The Family Stone
10/04	2	2	25.	Jean	Oliver
5/31	2	2	26.	Love (Can Make You Happy)	Mercy
9/27	1	2	27.	Green River	Creedence Clearwater Revival
11/22	1	2	28.	Take A Letter Maria	R.B. Greaves
5/03	1	2	29.	It's Your Thing	The Isley Brothers
11/29	1	2	30.	And When I Die	Blood, Sweat & Tears
6/28	1	2	31.	Bad Moon Rising	Creedence Clearwater Revival
3/29	1	2	(32.)	Traces	Classics IV Featuring Dennis Yost ✓
2/22	3	3	33.	Build Me Up Buttercup	The Foundations
10/04	2	3	34.	Little Woman	Bobby Sherman
2/01	2	3	35.	Worst That Could Happen	Brooklyn Bridge
3/29	2	3	(36.)	Time Of The Season	The Zombies ✓
7/12	2	3	37.	Good Morning Starshine	Oliver
11/15	2	3	38.	Something	The Beatles
1/11	1	3	39.	Wichita Lineman	Glen Campbell
12/20	1	3	40.	Down On The Corner	Creedence Clearwater Revival

TOP 40 HITS
1970

PK DATE	PK WKS	PK POS	RANK	TITLE	ARTIST
2/28	6	1	1.	Bridge Over Troubled Water	Simon & Garfunkel
10/17	5	1	2.	I'll Be There	The Jackson 5
1/03	4	1	3.	Raindrops Keep Fallin' On My Head	B.J. Thomas
7/25	4	1	4.	(They Long To Be) Close To You	Carpenters
12/26	4	1	5.	My Sweet Lord	George Harrison
11/21	3	1	6.	I Think I Love You	The Partridge Family
9/19	3	1	7.	Ain't No Mountain High Enough	Diana Ross
5/09	3	1	8.	American Woman	The Guess Who
8/29	3	1	9.	War	Edwin Starr
4/11	2	1	10.	Let It Be	The Beatles
12/12	2	1	11.	The Tears Of A Clown	Smokey Robinson & The Miracles
7/11	2	1	12.	Mama Told Me (Not To Come)	Three Dog Night
4/25	2	1	13.	ABC	The Jackson 5
6/27	2	1	14.	The Love You Save	The Jackson 5
2/14	2	1	15.	Thank You (Falettinme Be Mice Elf Agin)	Sly & The Family Stone
5/30	2	1	16.	Everything Is Beautiful	Ray Stevens
6/13	2	1	17.	The Long And Winding Road	The Beatles
8/22	1	1	18.	Make It With You	Bread
1/31	1	1	19.	I Want You Back	The Jackson 5
2/07	1	1	20.	Venus	The Shocking Blue
10/10	1	1	21.	Cracklin' Rosie	Neil Diamond
10/31	4	2	22.	We've Only Just Begun	Carpenters
12/26	2	2	23.	One Less Bell To Answer	The 5th Dimension
6/06	2	2	24.	Which Way You Goin' Billy?	The Poppy Family/Susan Jacks
3/07	2	2	25.	Travelin' Band	Creedence Clearwater Revival
10/03	1	2	26.	Lookin' Out My Back Door	Creedence Clearwater Revival
2/21	1	2	27.	Hey There Lonely Girl	Eddie Holman
3/21	1	2	28.	The Rapper	The Jaggerz
5/23	1	2	29.	Vehicle	The Ides Of March √
6/27	3	3	30.	Ball Of Confusion (That's What The World Is Today)	The Temptations
10/31	3	3	31.	Fire And Rain	James Taylor
4/18	3	3	32.	Spirit In The Sky	Norman Greenbaum
3/28	3	3	33.	Instant Karma (We All Shine On)	John Ono Lennon
12/05	2	3	34.	Gypsy Woman	Brian Hyland
10/03	2	3	35.	Candida	Dawn
10/17	2	3	36.	Green-Eyed Lady	Sugarloaf
8/08	2	3	37.	Signed, Sealed, Delivered I'm Yours	Stevie Wonder
5/30	2	3	38.	Love On A Two-Way Street	The Moments
7/25	1	3	39.	Band Of Gold	Freda Payne
8/22	1	3	40.	Spill The Wine	Eric Burdon & War

"BETH"

NB-863

KISS

SMASH

A rock steady PRODUCTION INC.

Produced by
Bob Ezrin

A   new single from the album "I'm Nearly Famous" PIG-2210
Produced by Bruce Welch

"DEVIL WOMAN"
PIG-40574
CLIFF RICHARD

TOP 40 HITS
1971

PK DATE	PK WKS	PK POS	RANK	TITLE	ARTIST
4/17	6	1	1.	Joy To The World	Three Dog Night
10/02	5	1	2.	Maggie May	Rod Stewart
6/19	5	1	3.	It's Too Late	Carole King
2/13	5	1	4.	One Bad Apple	The Osmonds
8/07	4	1	5.	How Can You Mend A Broken Heart	The Bee Gees
1/23	3	1	6.	Knock Three Times	Dawn
12/25	3	1	7.	Brand New Key	Melanie
9/11	3	1	8.	Go Away Little Girl	Donny Osmond
12/04	3	1	9.	Family Affair	Sly & The Family Stone
11/06	2	1	10.	Gypsys, Tramps & Thieves	Cher
4/03	2	1	11.	Just My Imagination (Running Away With Me)	The Temptations
11/20	2	1	12.	Theme From Shaft	Isaac Hayes
3/20	2	1	13.	Me And Bobby McGee	Janis Joplin
5/29	2	1	14.	Brown Sugar	The Rolling Stones
7/24	1	1	15.	Indian Reservation	Raiders
6/12	1	1	16.	Want Ads	The Honey Cone
7/31	1	1	17.	You've Got A Friend	James Taylor
9/04	1	1	18.	Uncle Albert/Admiral Halsey	Paul & Linda McCartney
4/10	3	2	19.	What's Going On	Marvin Gaye
5/08	3	2	20.	Never Can Say Goodbye	The Jackson 5
8/14	2	2	21.	Mr. Big Stuff	Jean Knight
10/16	2	2	22.	Superstar	Carpenters
6/19	2	2	23.	Rainy Days And Mondays	Carpenters
9/11	2	2	24.	Spanish Harlem	Aretha Franklin
2/27	2	2	25.	Mama's Pearl	The Jackson 5
8/28	1	2	26.	Take Me Home, Country Roads	John Denver
3/20	1	2	27.	She's A Lady	Tom Jones
5/01	1	2	28.	Put Your Hand In The Hand	Ocean
10/16	3	3	29.	Yo-Yo	The Osmonds
12/11	2	3	30.	Have You Seen Her	Chi-Lites
7/03	2	3	31.	Treat Her Like A Lady	Cornelius Brothers & Sister Rose
3/13	2	3	32.	For All We Know	Carpenters
2/13	2	3	33.	Rose Garden	Lynn Anderson
9/04	2	3	34.	Smiling Faces Sometimes	The Undisputed Truth
9/18	2	3	35.	Ain't No Sunshine	Bill Withers
11/13	2	3	36.	Imagine	John Lennon Plastic Ono Band
11/27	2	3	37.	Baby I'm-A Want You	Bread
10/02	1	3	38.	The Night They Drove Old Dixie Down	Joan Baez
1/30	1	3	39.	Lonely Days	Bee Gees
8/28	1	3	40.	Signs	Five Man Electrical Band

TOP 40 HITS
1972

PK DATE	PK WKS	PK POS	RANK	TITLE	ARTIST
4/15	6	1	1.	The First Time Ever I Saw Your Face	Roberta Flack
7/29	6	1	2.	Alone Again (Naturally)	Gilbert O'Sullivan
1/15	4	1	3.	American Pie - Parts I & II	Don McLean
2/19	4	1	4.	Without You	Nilsson
11/04	4	1	5.	I Can See Clearly Now	Johnny Nash
3/25	3	1	6.	A Horse With No Name	America
9/23	3	1	7.	Baby Don't Get Hooked On Me	Mac Davis
12/16	3	1	8.	Me And Mrs. Jones	Billy Paul
6/10	3	1	9.	The Candy Man	Sammy Davis, Jr.
7/08	3	1	10.	Lean On Me	Bill Withers
10/21	2	1	11.	My Ding-A-Ling	Chuck Berry
8/26	1	1	12.	Brandy (You're A Fine Girl)	Looking Glass
2/12	1	1	13.	Let's Stay Together	Al Green
12/09	1	1	14.	I Am Woman	Helen Reddy
6/03	1	1	15.	I'll Take You There	The Staple Singers
3/18	1	1	16.	Heart Of Gold	Neil Young
5/27	1	1	17.	Oh Girl	Chi-Lites
10/14	1	1	18.	Ben	Michael Jackson
12/02	1	1	19.	Papa Was A Rollin' Stone	The Temptations
7/01	1	1	20.	Song Sung Blue	Neil Diamond
9/16	1	1	21.	Black & White	Three Dog Night
5/06	2	2	22.	I Gotcha	Joe Tex
9/02	2	2	23.	Long Cool Woman (In A Black Dress)	The Hollies
7/15	2	2	24.	Too Late To Turn Back Now	Cornelius Brothers & Sister Rose
4/22	2	2	25.	Rockin' Robin	Michael Jackson
11/04	2	2	26.	Nights In White Satin	The Moody Blues
12/30	2	2	27.	Clair	Gilbert O'Sullivan
2/26	2	2	28.	Hurting Each Other	Carpenters
11/18	2	2	29.	I'd Love You To Want Me	Lobo
10/14	2	2	30.	Use Me	Bill Withers
7/08	1	2	31.	Outa-Space	Billy Preston
10/28	1	2	32.	Burning Love	Elvis Presley
3/11	3	3	33.	The Lion Sleeps Tonight	Robert John
8/05	2	3	34.	(If Loving You Is Wrong) I Don't Want To Be Right	Luther Ingram
2/26	2	3	35.	Precious And Few	Climax
12/23	2	3	36.	You Ought To Be With Me	Al Green
9/02	2	3	37.	I'm Still In Love With You	Al Green
12/09	2	3	38.	If You Don't Know Me By Now	Harold Melvin & The Bluenotes
11/18	2	3	39.	I'll Be Around	The Spinners
9/23	2	3	40.	Saturday In The Park	Chicago

TOP 40 HITS
1973

PK DATE	PK WKS	PK POS	RANK	TITLE	ARTIST
2/24	5	1	1.	Killing Me Softly With His Song	Roberta Flack
4/21	4	1	2.	Tie A Yellow Ribbon Round The Ole Oak Tree	Dawn Featuring Tony Orlando
6/02	4	1	3.	My Love	Paul McCartney & Wings
1/06	3	1	4.	You're So Vain	Carly Simon
2/03	3	1	5.	Crocodile Rock	Elton John
9/08	2	1	6.	Let's Get It On	Marvin Gaye
11/10	2	1	7.	Keep On Truckin' (Part 1)	Eddie Kendricks
7/21	2	1	8.	Bad, Bad Leroy Brown	Jim Croce
12/01	2	1	9.	Top Of The World	Carpenters
10/27	2	1	10.	Midnight Train To Georgia	Gladys Knight & The Pips
8/25	2	1	11.	Brother Louie	Stories
7/07	2	1	12.	Will It Go Round In Circles	Billy Preston
10/06	2	1	13.	Half-Breed	Cher
4/07	2	1	14.	The Night The Lights Went Out In Georgia	Vicki Lawrence
12/29	2	1	15.	Time In A Bottle	Jim Croce
12/15	2	1	16.	The Most Beautiful Girl	Charlie Rich
8/04	2	1	17.	The Morning After	Maureen McGovern
8/18	1	1	18.	Touch Me In The Morning	Diana Ross
9/15	1	1	19.	Delta Dawn	Helen Reddy
5/26	1	1	20.	Frankenstein	The Edgar Winter Group
5/19	1	1	21.	You Are The Sunshine Of My Life	Stevie Wonder
10/20	1	1	22.	Angie	The Rolling Stones
6/30	1	1	23.	Give Me Love - (Give Me Peace On Earth)	George Harrison
9/29	1	1	24.	We're An American Band	Grand Funk
1/27	1	1	25.	Superstition	Stevie Wonder
3/24	1	1	26.	Love Train	O'Jays
11/24	1	1	27.	Photograph	Ringo Starr
2/24	4	2	28.	Dueling Banjos	Eric Weissberg & Steve Mandell
12/08	3	2	29.	Goodbye Yellow Brick Road	Elton John
8/11	3	2	30.	Live And Let Die	Wings
6/16	2	2	31.	Playground In My Mind	Clint Holmes
7/07	2	2	32.	Kodachrome	Paul Simon
4/07	2	2	33.	Neither One Of Us (Wants To Be The First To Say Goodbye)	Gladys Knight & The Pips
4/28	2	2	34.	The Cisco Kid	War
10/06	1	2	35.	Loves Me Like A Rock	Paul Simon
6/02	1	2	36.	Daniel	Elton John
10/13	1	2	37.	Ramblin Man	The Allman Brothers Band
7/28	1	2	38.	Yesterday Once More	Carpenters
3/31	1	2	39.	Also Sprach Zarathustra (2001)	Deodato
5/05	3	3	40.	Little Willy	The Sweet

TOP 40 HITS
1974

PK DATE	PK WKS	PK POS	RANK	TITLE	ARTIST
2/02	3	1	1.	The Way We Were	Barbra Streisand
3/02	3	1	2.	Seasons In The Sun	Terry Jacks
5/18	3	1	3.	The Streak	Ray Stevens
8/24	3	1	4.	(You're) Having My Baby	Paul Anka
12/07	2	1	5.	Kung Fu Fighting	Carl Douglas
6/15	2	1	6.	Billy, Don't Be A Hero	Bo Donaldson & The Heywoods
7/27	2	1	7.	Annie's Song	John Denver
5/04	2	1	8.	The Loco-Motion	Grand Funk
4/20	2	1	9.	TSOP (The Sound Of Philadelphia)	MFSB with The Three Degrees
11/23	2	1	10.	I Can Help	Billy Swan
7/13	2	1	11.	Rock Your Baby	George McCrae
10/05	2	1	12.	I Honestly Love You	Olivia Newton-John
4/13	1	1	13.	Bennie And The Jets	Elton John
1/12	1	1	14.	The Joker	Steve Miller Band
10/26	1	1	15.	Then Came You	Dionne Warwicke & Spinners
2/09	1	1	16.	Love's Theme	Love Unlimited Orchestra
1/19	1	1	17.	Show And Tell	Al Wilson
11/02	1	1	18.	You Haven't Done Nothin	Stevie Wonder
10/19	1	1	19.	Nothing From Nothing	Billy Preston
4/06	1	1	20.	Hooked On A Feeling	Blue Swede
3/30	1	1	21.	Sunshine On My Shoulders	John Denver
6/08	1	1	22.	Band On The Run	Paul McCartney & Wings
1/26	1	1	23.	You're Sixteen	Ringo Starr
6/29	1	1	24.	Sundown	Gordon Lightfoot
9/28	1	1	25.	Rock Me Gently	Andy Kim
12/28	1	1	26.	Angie Baby	Helen Reddy
8/10	1	1	27.	Feel Like Makin' Love	Roberta Flack
12/21	1	1	28.	Cat's In The Cradle	Harry Chapin
3/23	1	1	29.	Dark Lady	Cher
8/17	1	1	30.	The Night Chicago Died	Paper Lace
11/09	1	1	31.	You Ain't Seen Nothing Yet	Bachman-Turner Overdrive
7/06	1	1	32.	Rock The Boat	The Hues Corporation
9/14	1	1	33.	I Shot The Sheriff	Eric Clapton
9/21	1	1	34.	Can't Get Enough Of Your Love, Babe	Barry White
11/16	1	1	35.	Whatever Gets You Thru The Night	John Lennon/Plastic Ono Band
5/18	2	2	36.	Dancing Machine	The Jackson 5
6/15	2	2	37.	You Make Me Feel Brand New	The Stylistics
11/16	2	2	38.	Do It ('Til You're Satisfied)	B.T. Express
3/09	2	2	39.	Boogie Down	Eddie Kendricks
7/27	2	2	40.	Don't Let The Sun Go Down On Me	Elton John

TOP 40 HITS
1975

PK DATE	PK WKS	PK POS	RANK	TITLE	ARTIST
6/21	4	1	1.	Love Will Keep Us Together	The Captain & Tennille
11/29	3	1	2.	Fly, Robin, Fly	Silver Convention
11/01	3	1	3.	Island Girl	Elton John
5/03	3	1	4.	He Don't Love You (Like I Love You)	Tony Orlando & Dawn
10/11	3	1	5.	Bad Blood	Neil Sedaka
9/06	2	1	6.	Rhinestone Cowboy	Glen Campbell
4/12	2	1	7.	Philadelphia Freedom	The Elton John Band
11/22	2	1	8.	That's The Way (I Like It)	KC & The Sunshine Band
8/09	2	1	9.	Jive Talkin'	Bee Gees
9/20	2	1	10.	Fame	David Bowie
1/04	2	1	11.	Lucy In The Sky With Diamonds	Elton John
8/02	1	1	12.	One Of These Nights	Eagles
5/31	1	1	13.	Before The Next Teardrop Falls	Freddy Fender
3/22	1	1	14.	My Eyes Adored You	Frankie Valli
4/05	1	1	15.	Lovin' You	Minnie Riperton
2/01	1	1	16.	Laughter In The Rain	Neil Sedaka
4/26	1	1	17.	(Hey Won't You Play) Another Somebody Done Somebody Wrong Song	B.J. Thomas
3/29	1	1	18.	Lady Marmalade	LaBelle
2/22	1	1	19.	Pick Up The Pieces	AWB (Average White Band)
7/26	1	1	20.	The Hustle	Van McCoy
3/15	1	1	21.	Black Water	The Doobie Brothers
12/27	1	1	22.	Let's Do It Again	The Staple Singers
3/08	1	1	23.	Have You Never Been Mellow	Olivia Newton-John
7/19	1	1	24.	Listen To What The Man Said	Wings
3/01	1	1	25.	Best Of My Love	The Eagles
8/23	1	1	26.	Fallin' In Love	Hamilton, Joe Frank & Reynolds
6/07	1	1	27.	Thank God I'm A Country Boy	John Denver
5/24	1	1	28.	Shining Star	Earth, Wind & Fire
1/25	1	1	29.	Please Mr. Postman	Carpenters
1/18	1	1	30.	Mandy	Barry Manilow
2/15	1	1	31.	You're No Good	Linda Ronstadt
9/27	1	1	32.	I'm Sorry	John Denver
2/08	1	1	33.	Fire	Ohio Players
6/14	1	1	34.	Sister Golden Hair	America
8/30	1	1	35.	Get Down Tonight	K.C. & The Sunshine Band
10/11	4	2	36.	Calypso	John Denver
7/26	3	2	37.	I'm Not In Love	10cc
6/21	2	2	38.	When Will I Be Loved	Linda Ronstadt
1/04	2	2	39.	You're The First, The Last, My Everything	Barry White
11/08	2	2	40.	Lyin' Eyes	The Eagles

TOP 40 HITS
1976

PK DATE	PK WKS	PK POS	RANK	TITLE	ARTIST
11/13	8	1	1.	Tonight's The Night (Gonna Be Alright)	Rod Stewart
5/22	5	1	2.	Silly Love Songs	Wings
8/07	4	1	3.	Don't Go Breaking My Heart	Elton John & Kiki Dee
4/03	4	1	4.	Disco Lady	Johnnie Taylor
9/18	3	1	5.	Play That Funky Music	Wild Cherry
3/13	3	1	6.	December, 1963 (Oh, What a Night)	The Four Seasons
2/07	3	1	7.	50 Ways To Leave Your Lover	Paul Simon
7/24	2	1	8.	Kiss And Say Goodbye	Manhattans
10/23	2	1	9.	If You Leave Me Now	Chicago
5/29	2	1	10.	Love Hangover	Diana Ross
7/10	2	1	11.	Afternoon Delight	Starland Vocal Band
9/11	1	1	12.	(Shake, Shake, Shake) Shake Your Booty	KC & The Sunshine Band
10/09	1	1	13.	A Fifth Of Beethoven	Walter Murphy/Big Apple Band
10/16	1	1	14.	Disco Duck (Part 1)	Rick Dees & His Cast Of Idiots
1/17	1	1	15.	I Write The Songs	Barry Manilow
1/31	1	1	16.	Love Rollercoaster	Ohio Players
5/15	1	1	17.	Boogie Fever	Sylvers
1/24	1	1	18.	Theme From Mahogany (Do You Know Where You're Going To)	Diana Ross
9/04	1	1	19.	You Should Be Dancing	Bee Gees
5/01	1	1	20.	Let Your Love Flow	Bellamy Brothers
1/10	1	1	21.	Convoy	C.W. McCall
5/08	1	1	22.	Welcome Back	John Sebastian
3/06	1	1	23.	Love Machine (Part 1)	The Miracles
2/28	1	1	24.	Theme From S.W.A.T.	Rhythm Heritage
1/03	1	1	25.	Saturday Night	Bay City Rollers
11/06	1	1	26.	Rock'n Me	Steve Miller
12/04	3	2	27.	The Rubberband Man	Spinners
6/12	3	2	28.	Get Up And Boogie (That's Right)	Silver Convention
3/27	3	2	29.	Dream Weaver	Gary Wright
3/06	3	2	30.	All By Myself	Eric Carmen
9/25	2	2	31.	I'd Really Love To See You Tonight	England Dan & John Ford Coley
5/01	2	2	32.	Right Back Where We Started From	Maxine Nightingale
9/04	2	2	33.	You'll Never Find Another Love Like Mine	Lou Rawls
7/31	2	2	34.	Love Is Alive	Gary Wright
2/07	2	2	35.	Love To Love You Baby	Donna Summer
1/20	2	2	36.	The Wreck Of The Edmund Fitzgerald	Gordon Lightfoot
1/20	4	3	37.	Love So Right	Bee Gees
6/12	4	3	38.	Misty Blue	Dorthy Moore
8/14	4	3	39.	Let 'Em In	Wings
2/07	3	3	40.	You Sexy Thing	Hot Chocolate

TOP 40 HITS
1977

PK DATE	PK WKS	PK POS	RANK	TITLE	ARTIST
10/15	10	1	1.	You Light Up My Life	Debby Boone
8/20	5	1	2.	Best Of My Love	Emotions
7/30	4	1	3.	I Just Want To Be Your Everything	Andy Gibb
12/24	3	1	4.	How Deep Is Your Love	Bee Gees
3/05	3	1	5.	Love Theme From "A Star Is Born" (Evergreen)	Barbra Streisand
5/21	3	1	6.	Sir Duke	Stevie Wonder
2/05	2	1	7.	Torn Between Two Lovers	Mary MacGregor
3/26	2	1	8.	Rich Girl	Daryl Hall & John Oates
10/01	2	1	9.	Star Wars Theme/Cantina Band	Meco
6/25	1	1	10.	Got To Give It Up (Pt. I)	Marvin Gaye
1/29	1	1	11.	Car Wash	Rose Royce
1/08	1	1	12.	You Don't Have To Be A Star (To Be In My Show)	Marilyn McCoo & Billy Davis, Jr.
4/23	1	1	13.	Don't Leave Me This Way	Thelma Houston
1/15	1	1	14.	You Make Me Feel Like Dancing	Leo Sayer
4/09	1	1	15.	Dancing Queen	Abba
4/30	1	1	16.	Southern Nights	Glen Campbell
2/19	1	1	17.	Blinded By The Light	Manfred Mann's Earth Band
5/07	1	1	18.	Hotel California	Eagles
1/22	1	1	19.	I Wish	Stevie Wonder
7/02	1	1	20.	Gonna Fly Now	Bill Conti
7/09	1	1	21.	Undercover Angel	Alan O'Day
5/14	1	1	22.	When I Need You	Leo Sayer
4/16	1	1	23.	Don't Give Up On Us	David Soul
6/18	1	1	24.	Dreams	Fleetwood Mac
2/26	1	1	25.	New Kid In Town	Eagles
7/16	1	1	26.	Da Doo Ron Ron	Shaun Cassidy
6/11	1	1	27.	I'm Your Boogie Man	KC & The Sunshine Band
7/23	1	1	28.	Looks Like We Made It	Barry Manilow
11/26	3	2	29.	Don't It Make My Brown Eyes Blue	Crystal Gayle
10/22	3	2	30.	Nobody Does It Better	Carly Simon
10/01	3	2	31.	Keep It Comin' Love	KC & The Sunshine Band
7/30	3	2	32.	I'm In You	Peter Frampton
11/12	2	2	33.	Boogie Nights	Heatwave
3/12	2	2	34.	Fly Like An Eagle	Steve Miller
9/17	2	2	35.	Float On	The Floaters
9/10	1	2	36.	(Your Love Has Lifted Me) Higher And Higher	Rita Coolidge
12/17	4	3	37.	Blue Bayou	Linda Ronstadt
1/29	2	3	38.	Dazz	Brick
10/22	2	3	39.	That's Rock 'N' Roll	Shaun Cassidy
9/24	2	3	40.	Don't Stop	Fleetwood Mac

TOP 40 HITS
1978

PK DATE	PK WKS	PK POS	RANK	TITLE	ARTIST
3/18	8	1	1.	Night Fever	Bee Gees
6/17	7	1	2.	Shadow Dancing	Andy Gibb
12/09	6	1	3.	Le Freak	Chic
2/04	4	1	4.	Stayin' Alive	Bee Gees
9/30	4	1	5.	Kiss You All Over	Exile
9/09	3	1	6.	Boogie Oogie Oogie	A Taste Of Honey
1/14	3	1	7.	Baby Come Back	Player
11/11	3	1	8.	MacArthur Park	Donna Summer
3/04	2	1	9.	(Love Is) Thicker Than Water	Andy Gibb
8/12	2	1	10.	Three Times A Lady	Commodores
12/02	2	1	11.	You Don't Bring Me Flowers	Barbra Streisand & Neil Diamond
8/26	2	1	12.	Grease	Frankie Valli
5/20	2	1	13.	With A Little Luck	Wings
5/13	1	1	14.	If I Can't Have You	Yvonne Elliman
10/28	1	1	15.	Hot Child In The City	Nick Gilder
6/10	1	1	16.	You're The One That I Want	John Travolta & Olivia Newton-John
8/05	1	1	17.	Miss You	The Rolling Stones
11/04	1	1	18.	You Needed Me	Anne Murray
6/03	1	1	19.	Too Much, Too Little, Too Late	Johnny Mathis/Deniece Williams
6/24	6	2	20.	Baker Street	Gerry Rafferty
1/28	3	2	21.	Short People	Randy Newman
5/13	2	2	22.	The Closer I Get To You	Roberta Flack with Donny Hathaway
11/18	2	2	23.	Double Vision	Foreigner
4/01	3	3	24.	Lay Down Sally	Eric Clapton
4/22	3	3	25.	Can't Smile Without You	Barry Manilow
11/18	3	3	26.	How Much I Feel	Ambrosia
3/18	2	3	27.	Emotion	Samantha Sang
2/18	2	3	28.	Just The Way You Are	Billy Joel
3/04	2	3	29.	Sometimes When We Touch	Dan Hill
9/23	2	3	30.	Hopelessly Devoted To You	Olivia Newton-John
7/08	2	3	31.	Take A Chance On Me	Abba
9/09	2	3	32.	Hot Blooded	Foreigner
8/12	2	3	33.	Last Dance	Donna Summer
10/28	2	3	34.	Reminiscing	Little River Band
6/24	2	3	35.	It's A Heartache	Bonnie Tyler
1/14	2	3	36.	Here You Come Again	Dolly Parton
2/04	3	4	37.	We Are The Champions	Queen
1/14	3	4	38.	You're In My Heart (The Final Acclaim)	Rod Stewart
12/09	2	4	39.	I Just Wanna Stop	Gino Vannelli
7/08	2	4	40.	Use Ta Be My Girl	The O'Jays

WAR

Why can't we be friends?

UAXW-629X

A NEW SINGLE FROM WAR.

Produced by Jerry Goldstein in association with Lonnie Jordan and Howard Scott for Far Out Productions   A Far Out Production on United Artists Records & Tapes

TOP 40 HITS
1979

PK DATE	PK WKS	PK POS	RANK	TITLE	ARTIST
8/25	6	1	1.	My Sharona	The Knack
7/14	5	1	2.	Bad Girls	Donna Summer
2/10	4	1	3.	Da Ya Think I'm Sexy?	Rod Stewart
5/05	4	1	4.	Reunited	Peaches & Herb
6/02	3	1	5.	Hot Stuff	Donna Summer
3/10	3	1	6.	I Will Survive	Gloria Gaynor
12/22	3	1	7.	Escape (The Pina Colada Song)	Rupert Holmes
6/30	2	1	8.	Ring My Bell	Anita Ward
12/08	2	1	9.	Babe	Styx
1/06	2	1	10.	Too Much Heaven	Bee Gees
10/20	2	1	11.	Rise	Herb Alpert
3/24	2	1	12.	Tragedy	Bee Gees
11/24	2	1	13.	No More Tears (Enough Is Enough)	Barbra Streisand/Donna Summer
11/17	1	1	14.	Still	Commodores
11/03	1	1	15.	Pop Muzik	M
10/06	1	1	16.	Sad Eyes	Robert John
4/14	1	1	17.	What A Fool Believes	The Doobie Brothers
8/18	1	1	18.	Good Times	Chic
11/10	1	1	19.	Heartache Tonight	Eagles
4/28	1	1	20.	Heart Of Glass	Blondie
4/21	1	1	21.	Knock On Wood	Amii Stewart
10/13	1	1	22.	Don't Stop 'Til You Get Enough	Michael Jackson
6/09	1	1	23.	Love You Inside Out	Bee Gees
2/03	3	2	24.	Y.M.C.A.	Village People
11/10	2	2	25.	Dim All The Lights	Donna Summer
9/15	2	2	26.	After The Love Has Gone	Earth, Wind & Fire
2/24	2	2	27.	Fire	Pointer Sisters
6/16	2	2	28.	We Are Family	Sister Sledge
8/11	4	3	29.	The Main Event/Fight	Barbra Streisand
1/06	3	3	30.	My Life	Billy Joel
2/17	2	3	31.	A Little More Love	Olivia Newton-John
9/15	2	3	32.	The Devil Went Down To Georgia	The Charlie Daniels Band
5/19	2	3	33.	In The Navy	Village People
5/05	1	3	34.	Music Box Dancer	Frank Mills
12/22	4	4	35.	Send One Your Love	Stevie Wonder
3/17	3	4	36.	Heaven Knows	Donna Summer with Brooklyn Dreams
5/12	2	4	37.	Stumblin' In	Suzi Quatro & Chris Norman
10/13	2	4	38.	Sail On	Commodores
4/07	2	4	39.	Sultans Of Swing	Dire Straits
6/16	2	4	40.	Just When I Needed You Most	Randy Vanwarmer

TOP 40 HITS
1980

PK DATE	PK WKS	PK POS	RANK	TITLE	ARTIST
11/15	6	1	1.	Lady	Kenny Rogers
4/19	6	1	2.	Call Me	Blondie
12/27	5	1	3.	(Just Like) Starting Over	John Lennon
9/06	4	1	4.	Upside Down	Diana Ross
3/22	4	1	5.	Another Brick In The Wall (Part II)	Pink Floyd
2/23	4	1	6.	Crazy Little Thing Called Love	Queen
1/19	4	1	7.	Rock With You	Michael Jackson
8/02	4	1	8.	Magic	Olivia Newton-John
5/31	4	1	9.	Funkytown	Lipps, Inc.
10/04	3	1	10.	Another One Bites The Dust	Queen
10/25	3	1	11.	Woman In Love	Barbra Streisand
6/28	3	1	12.	Coming Up (Live at Glasgow)	Paul McCartney & Wings
7/19	2	1	13.	It's Still Rock And Roll To Me	Billy Joel
2/16	1	1	14.	Do That To Me One More Time	The Captain & Tennille
1/05	1	1	15.	Please Don't Go	K.C. & The Sunshine Band
8/30	1	1	16.	Sailing	Christopher Cross
12/06	5	2	17.	More Than I Can Say	Leo Sayer
9/13	4	2	18.	All Out Of Love	Air Supply
4/26	4	2	19.	Ride Like The Wind	Christopher Cross
3/29	2	2	20.	Working My Way Back To You/Forgive Me, Girl	Spinners
3/01	2	2	21.	Yes, I'm Ready	Teri DeSario with K.C.
3/15	2	2	22.	Longer	Dan Fogelberg
7/19	4	3	23.	Little Jeannie	Elton John
1/26	4	3	24.	Coward Of The County	Kenny Rogers
5/03	4	3	25.	Lost In Love	Air Supply
6/28	3	3	26.	The Rose	Bette Midler
6/07	3	3	27.	Biggest Part Of Me	Ambrosia
11/15	3	3	28.	The Wanderer	Donna Summer
10/25	3	3	29.	He's So Shy	Pointer Sisters
9/06	2	3	30.	Emotional Rescue	The Rolling Stones
8/16	2	3	31.	Take Your Time (Do It Right) Part 1	The S.O.S. Band
3/08	4	4	32.	Desire	Andy Gibb
2/02	4	4	33.	Cruisin'	Smokey Robinson
4/19	4	4	34.	With You I'm Born Again	Billy Preston & Syreeta
7/19	3	4	35.	Cupid/I've Loved You For A Long Time	Spinners
5/24	3	4	36.	Don't Fall In Love With A Dreamer	Kenny Rogers with Kim Carnes
9/27	2	4	37.	Give Me The Night	George Benson
9/13	2	4	38.	Fame	Irene Cara
12/27	5	5	39.	Hungry Heart	Bruce Springsteen
12/06	3	5	40.	Master Blaster (Jammin')	Stevie Wonder

TOP 40 HITS
1981

PK DATE	PK WKS	PK POS	RANK	TITLE	ARTIST
11/21	10	1	1.	Physical	Olivia Newton-John
5/16	9	1	2.	Bette Davis Eyes	Kim Carnes
8/15	9	1	3.	Endless Love	Diana Ross & Lionel Richie
10/17	3	1	4.	Arthur's Theme (Best That You Can Do)	Christopher Cross
4/11	3	1	5.	Kiss On My List	Daryl Hall & John Oates
8/01	2	1	6.	Jessie's Girl	Rick Springfield
2/28	2	1	7.	I Love A Rainy Night	Eddie Rabbitt
2/21	2	1	8.	9 To 5	Dolly Parton
11/07	2	1	9.	Private Eyes	Daryl Hall & John Oates
3/28	2	1	10.	Rapture	Blondie
2/07	2	1	11.	Celebration	Kool & The Gang
5/02	2	1	12.	Morning Train (Nine To Five)	Sheena Easton
1/31	1	1	13.	The Tide Is High	Blondie
3/21	1	1	14.	Keep On Loving You	REO Speedwagon
6/20	1	1	15.	Stars on 45	Stars on 45
7/25	1	1	16.	The One That You Love	Air Supply
11/28	10	2	17.	Waiting For A Girl Like You	Foreigner
3/21	3	2	18.	Woman	John Lennon
10/31	3	2	19.	Start Me Up	The Rolling Stones
8/29	3	2	20.	Slow Hand	Pointer Sisters
5/02	3	2	21.	Just The Two Of Us	Grover Washington, Jr. with Bill Withers
1/10	3	2	22.	Love On The Rocks	Neil Diamond
5/23	3	2	23.	Being With You	Smokey Robinson
7/04	3	2	24.	All Those Years Ago	George Harrison
9/19	2	2	25.	Queen Of Hearts	Juice Newton
8/15	2	2	26.	Theme From "Greatest American Hero" (Believe It or Not)	Joey Scarbury
9/05	6	3	27.	Stop Draggin' My Heart Around	Stevie Nicks with Tom Petty & The Heartbreakers
12/19	5	3	28.	Let's Groove	Earth, Wind & Fire
3/21	4	3	29.	The Best Of Times	Styx
6/13	3	3	30.	Sukiyaki	A Taste Of Honey
8/15	2	3	31.	I Don't Need You	Kenny Rogers
1/10	2	3	32.	Guilty	Barbra Streisand & Barry Gibb
12/05	2	3	33.	Every Little Thing She Does Is Magic	The Police
9/05	4	4	34.	Urgent	Foreigner
5/02	4	4	35.	Angel Of The Morning	Juice Newton
10/17	4	4	36.	For Your Eyes Only	Sheena Easton
12/05	3	4	37.	Oh No	Commodores
10/03	2	4	38.	Who's Crying Now	Journey
6/20	2	4	39.	A Woman Needs Love (Just Like You Do)	Ray Parker Jr. & Raydio
9/05	5	5	40.	(There's) No Gettin' Over Me	Ronnie Milsap

TOP 40 HITS
1982

PK DATE	PK WKS	PK POS	RANK	TITLE	ARTIST
3/20	7	1	1.	I Love Rock 'N Roll	Joan Jett & The Blackhearts
5/15	7	1	2.	Ebony And Ivory	Paul McCartney/Stevie Wonder
7/24	6	1	3.	Eye Of The Tiger	Survivor
2/06	6	1	4.	Centerfold	The J. Geils Band
12/18	4	1	5.	Maneater	Daryl Hall & John Oates
10/02	4	1	6.	Jack & Diane	John Cougar
7/03	3	1	7.	Don't You Want Me	The Human League
11/06	3	1	8.	Up Where We Belong	Joe Cocker & Jennifer Warnes
9/04	2	1	9.	Abracadabra	The Steve Miller Band
9/11	2	1	10.	Hard To Say I'm Sorry	Chicago
11/27	2	1	11.	Truly	Lionel Richie
1/30	1	1	12.	I Can't Go For That (No Can Do)	Daryl Hall & John Oates
12/11	1	1	13.	Mickey	Toni Basil
10/30	1	1	14.	Who Can It Be Now?	Men At Work
5/08	1	1	15.	Chariots Of Fire - Titles	Vangelis
2/27	6	2	16.	Open Arms	Journey
7/03	5	2	17.	Rosanna	Toto
8/07	4	2	18.	Hurts So Good	John Cougar
5/22	4	2	19.	Don't Talk To Strangers	Rick Springfield
11/27	3	2	20.	Gloria	Laura Branigan
4/10	3	2	21.	We Got The Beat	Go-Go's
11/06	4	3	22.	Heart Attack	Olivia Newton-John
10/16	3	3	23.	Eye In The Sky	The Alan Parsons Project
5/22	3	3	24.	I've Never Been To Me	Charlene
2/13	2	3	25.	Harden My Heart	Quarterflash
7/24	7	4	26.	Hold Me	Fleetwood Mac
4/10	4	4	27.	Freeze-Frame	The J. Geils Band
3/20	3	4	28.	That Girl	Stevie Wonder
5/22	3	4	29.	867-5309/Jenny	Tommy Tutone
2/27	3	4	30.	Shake It Up	The Cars
10/23	3	4	31.	I Keep Forgettin' (Every Time You're Near)	Michael McDonald
6/26	3	4	32.	Heat Of The Moment	Asia
6/12	2	4	33.	The Other Woman	Ray Parker Jr.
11/13	4	5	34.	Heartlight	Neil Diamond
6/12	3	5	35.	Always On My Mind	Willie Nelson
9/18	3	5	36.	You Should Hear How She Talks About You	Melissa Manchester
4/03	3	5	37.	Make A Move On Me	Olivia Newton-John
9/04	2	5	38.	Even The Nights Are Better	Air Supply
3/20	2	5	39.	Sweet Dreams	Air Supply
7/17	2	5	40.	Let It Whip	Dazz Band

TOP 40 HITS
1983

PK DATE	PK WKS	PK POS	RANK	TITLE	ARTIST
7/09	8	1	1.	Every Breath You Take	The Police
3/05	7	1	2.	Billie Jean	Michael Jackson
5/28	6	1	3.	Flashdance...What A Feeling	Irene Cara
12/10	6	1	4.	Say Say Say	Paul McCartney & Michael Jackson
11/12	4	1	5.	All Night Long (All Night)	Lionel Richie
10/01	4	1	6.	Total Eclipse Of The Heart	Bonnie Tyler
1/15	4	1	7.	Down Under	Men At Work
4/30	3	1	8.	Beat It	Michael Jackson
10/29	2	1	9.	Islands In The Stream	Kenny Rogers & Dolly Parton
2/19	2	1	10.	Baby, Come To Me	Patti Austin with James Ingram
9/10	2	1	11.	Maniac	Michael Sembello
5/21	1	1	12.	Let's Dance	David Bowie
9/03	1	1	13.	Sweet Dreams (Are Made of This)	Eurythmics
9/24	1	1	14.	Tell Her About It	Billy Joel
2/05	1	1	15.	Africa	Toto
4/23	1	1	16.	Come On Eileen	Dexys Midnight Runners
7/02	5	2	17.	Electric Avenue	Eddy Grant
12/17	4	2	18.	Say It Isn't So	Daryl Hall - John Oates
2/26	4	2	19.	Shame On The Moon	Bob Seger/The Silver Bullet Band
1/08	3	2	20.	The Girl Is Mine	Michael Jackson/Paul McCartney
3/26	3	2	21.	Do You Really Want To Hurt Me	Culture Club
10/08	3	2	22.	Making Love Out Of Nothing At All	Air Supply
6/18	2	2	23.	Time (Clock Of The Heart)	Culture Club
5/07	1	2	24.	Jeopardy	Greg Kihn Band
11/12	5	3	25.	Uptown Girl	Billy Joel
9/10	4	3	26.	The Safety Dance	Men Without Hats
1/29	3	3	27.	Sexual Healing	Marvin Gaye
1/08	3	3	28.	Dirty Laundry	Don Henley
3/26	3	3	29.	Hungry Like The Wolf	Duran Duran
8/06	3	3	30.	She Works Hard For The Money	Donna Summer
12/24	3	3	31.	Union Of The Snake	Duran Duran
2/26	3	3	32.	Stray Cat Strut	Stray Cats
4/16	2	3	33.	Mr. Roboto	Styx
10/08	2	3	34.	King Of Pain	The Police
6/04	1	3	35.	Overkill	Men At Work
7/09	4	4	36.	Never Gonna Let You Go	Sergio Mendes
10/08	4	4	37.	True	Spandau Ballet
9/03	2	4	38.	Puttin' On The Ritz	Taco
3/26	2	4	39.	You Are	Lionel Richie
11/05	1	4	40.	One Thing Leads To Another	The Fixx

TOP 40 HITS
1984

PK DATE	PK WKS	PK POS	RANK	TITLE	ARTIST
12/22	6	1	1.	Like A Virgin	Madonna
7/07	5	1	2.	When Doves Cry	Prince
2/25	5	1	3.	Jump	Van Halen
3/31	3	1	4.	Footloose	Kenny Loggins
9/01	3	1	5.	What's Love Got To Do With It	Tina Turner
4/21	3	1	6.	Against All Odds (Take A Look At Me Now)	Phil Collins
10/13	3	1	7.	I Just Called To Say I Love You	Stevie Wonder
8/11	3	1	8.	Ghostbusters	Ray Parker Jr.
2/04	3	1	9.	Karma Chameleon	Culture Club
11/17	3	1	10.	Wake Me Up Before You Go-Go	Wham!
5/12	2	1	11.	Hello	Lionel Richie
1/21	2	1	12.	Owner Of A Lonely Heart	Yes
12/08	2	1	13.	Out Of Touch	Daryl Hall John Oates
6/09	2	1	14.	Time After Time	Cyndi Lauper
5/26	2	1	15.	Let's Hear It For The Boy	Deniece Williams
9/29	2	1	16.	Let's Go Crazy	Prince & The Revolution
6/23	2	1	17.	The Reflex	Duran Duran
11/03	2	1	18.	Caribbean Queen (No More Love On The Run)	Billy Ocean
9/22	1	1	19.	Missing You	John Waite
6/30	4	2	20.	Dancing In The Dark	Bruce Springsteen
12/15	4	2	21.	The Wild Boys	Duran Duran
3/24	3	2	22.	Somebody's Watching Me	Rockwell
3/10	2	2	23.	Girls Just Want To Have Fun	Cyndi Lauper
11/17	2	2	24.	Purple Rain	Prince & The Revolution
2/11	1	2	25.	Joanna	Kool & The Gang
3/03	1	2	26.	99 Luftballons	Nena
11/24	3	3	27.	I Feel For You	Chaka Khan
9/08	3	3	28.	She Bop	Cyndi Lauper
1/28	3	3	29.	Talking In Your Sleep	The Romantics
9/29	3	3	30.	Drive	The Cars
8/04	3	3	31.	State Of Shock	Jacksons
7/07	2	3	32.	Jump (For My Love)	Pointer Sisters
5/05	2	3	33.	Hold Me Now	Thompson Twins
8/25	2	3	34.	Stuck On You	Lionel Richie
10/20	2	3	35.	Hard Habit To Break	Chicago
6/09	1	3	36.	Oh Sherrie	Steve Perry
3/31	2	4	37.	Here Comes The Rain Again	Eurythmics
6/30	2	4	38.	Self Control	Laura Branigan
7/14	2	4	39.	Eyes Without A Face	Billy Idol
3/03	2	4	40.	Thriller	Michael Jackson

TOP 40 HITS
1985

PK DATE	PK WKS	PK POS	RANK	TITLE	ARTIST
12/21	4	1	1.	Say You, Say Me	Lionel Richie
4/13	4	1	2.	We Are The World	USA for Africa
2/16	3	1	3.	Careless Whisper	Wham! Featuring George Michael
3/09	3	1	4.	Can't Fight This Feeling	REO Speedwagon
9/21	3	1	5.	Money For Nothing	Dire Straits
8/03	3	1	6.	Shout	Tears For Fears
12/07	2	1	7.	Broken Wings	Mr. Mister
2/02	2	1	8.	I Want To Know What Love Is	Foreigner
8/24	2	1	9.	The Power Of Love	Huey Lewis & The News
6/08	2	1	10.	Everybody Wants To Rule The World	Tears For Fears
11/16	2	1	11.	We Built This City	Starship
9/07	2	1	12.	St. Elmo's Fire (Man In Motion)	John Parr
5/25	2	1	13.	Everything She Wants	Wham!
6/22	2	1	14.	Heaven	Bryan Adams
7/13	2	1	15.	A View To A Kill	Duran Duran
3/30	2	1	16.	One More Night	Phil Collins
11/30	1	1	17.	Separate Lives	Phil Collins & Marilyn Martin
5/11	1	1	18.	Crazy For You	Madonna
7/27	1	1	19.	Everytime You Go Away	Paul Young
5/18	1	1	20.	Don't You (Forget About Me)	Simple Minds
11/02	1	1	21.	Part-Time Lover	Stevie Wonder
10/19	1	1	22.	Take On Me	a-ha
10/26	1	1	23.	Saving All My Love For You	Whitney Houston
11/09	1	1	24.	Miami Vice Theme	Jan Hammer
7/06	1	1	25.	Sussudio	Phil Collins
10/12	1	1	26.	Oh Sheila	Ready For The World
12/28	3	2	27.	Party All The Time	Eddie Murphy
9/21	3	2	28.	Cherish	Kool & The Gang
2/02	2	2	29.	Easy Lover	Philip Bailey/Phil Collins
11/16	2	2	30.	You Belong To The City	Glenn Frey
1/12	2	2	31.	All I Need	Jack Wagner
3/23	2	2	32.	Material Girl	Madonna
2/23	1	2	33.	Loverboy	Billy Ocean
7/20	1	2	34.	Raspberry Beret	Prince & The Revolution
3/16	1	2	35.	The Heat Is On	Glenn Frey
9/14	1	2	36.	We Don't Need Another Hero (Thunderdome)	Tina Turner
6/01	3	3	37.	Axel F	Harold Faltermeyer
4/27	2	3	38.	Rhythm Of The Night	DeBarge
12/28	2	3	39.	Alive & Kicking	Simple Minds
1/19	2	3	40.	You're The Inspiration	Chicago

TOP 40 HITS
1986

PK DATE	PK WKS	PK POS	RANK	TITLE	ARTIST
1/18	4	1	1.	That's What Friends Are For	Dionne & Friends
12/20	4	1	2.	Walk Like An Egyptian	Bangles
6/14	3	1	3.	On My Own	Patti LaBelle & Michael McDonald
5/17	3	1	4.	Greatest Love Of All	Whitney Houston
9/20	3	1	5.	Stuck With You	Huey Lewis & The News
3/29	3	1	6.	Rock Me Amadeus	Falco
3/01	2	1	7.	Kyrie	Mr. Mister
4/19	2	1	8.	Kiss	Prince & The Revolution
8/16	2	1	9.	Papa Don't Preach	Madonna
2/15	2	1	10.	How Will I Know	Whitney Houston
8/02	2	1	11.	Glory Of Love	Peter Cetera
10/11	2	1	12.	When I Think Of You	Janet Jackson
10/25	2	1	13.	True Colors	Cyndi Lauper
11/08	2	1	14.	Amanda	Boston
12/13	1	1	15.	The Way It Is	Bruce Hornsby & The Range
11/22	1	1	16.	Human	Human League
5/03	1	1	17.	Addicted To Love	Robert Palmer
7/05	1	1	18.	There'll Be Sad Songs (To Make You Cry)	Billy Ocean
7/26	1	1	19.	Sledgehammer	Peter Gabriel
5/10	1	1	20.	West End Girls	Pet Shop Boys
9/13	1	1	21.	Take My Breath Away	Berlin
3/15	1	1	22.	Sara	Starship
9/06	1	1	23.	Venus	Bananarama
12/06	1	1	24.	The Next Time I Fall	Peter Cetera w/Amy Grant
11/29	1	1	25.	You Give Love A Bad Name	Bon Jovi
7/12	1	1	26.	Holding Back The Years	Simply Red
8/30	1	1	27.	Higher Love	Steve Winwood
3/22	1	1	28.	These Dreams	Heart
6/07	1	1	29.	Live To Tell	Madonna
7/19	1	1	30.	Invisible Touch	Genesis
10/18	3	2	31.	Typical Male	Tina Turner
9/13	2	2	32.	Dancing On The Ceiling	Lionel Richie
12/27	2	2	33.	Everybody Have Fun Tonight	Wang Chung
9/27	2	2	34.	Friends And Lovers	Gloria Loring & Carl Anderson
2/01	2	2	35.	Burning Heart	Survivor
7/26	1	2	36.	Danger Zone	Kenny Loggins
10/11	1	2	37.	Don't Forget Me (When I'm Gone)	Glass Tiger
2/15	1	2	38.	When The Going Gets Tough, The Tough Get Going	Billy Ocean
4/19	1	2	39.	Manic Monday	Bangles
11/08	1	2	40.	I Didn't Mean To Turn You On	Robert Palmer

CAT STEVENS NEW SINGLE. PEACE TRAIN

It's Cat's new single from his even newer album, "Teaser and the Fire Cat." **Peace Train, AM1291 on A&M Records and Tapes.**

PRODUCED BY PAUL SAMWELL-SMITH

The M.O.R. Smash
"THE CANDY MAN"
[K-14320]
by **SAMMY DAVIS JR.**
also breaking Top 40 in
Philadelphia, Detroit, Seattle, Baltimore,
Washington D.C. and Hartford
from his new album
"SAMMY DAVIS JR. NOW"
[SE-4832]

ALTO
PRODUCTIONS

©1972 MGM Record Corp.

MGM
RECORDS

TOP 40 HITS
1987

PK DATE	PK WKS	PK POS	RANK	TITLE	ARTIST
12/12	4	1	1.	Faith	George Michael
2/14	4	1	2.	Livin' On A Prayer	Bon Jovi
7/11	3	1	3.	Alone	Heart
5/16	3	1	4.	With Or Without You	U2
8/29	3	1	5.	La Bamba	Los Lobos
6/27	2	1	6.	I Wanna Dance With Somebody (Who Loves Me)	Whitney Houston
4/04	2	1	7.	Nothing's Gonna Stop Us Now	Starship
8/08	2	1	8.	I Still Haven't Found What I'm Looking For	U2
9/26	2	1	9.	Didn't We Almost Have It All	Whitney Houston
4/18	2	1	10.	I Knew You Were Waiting (For Me)	Aretha Franklin & George Michael
1/24	2	1	11.	At This Moment	Billy Vera & The Beaters
11/07	2	1	12.	I Think We're Alone Now	Tiffany
5/02	2	1	13.	(I Just) Died In Your Arms	Cutting Crew
3/21	2	1	14.	Lean On Me	Club Nouveau
10/24	2	1	15.	Bad	Michael Jackson
1/17	1	1	16.	Shake You Down	Gregory Abbott
10/10	1	1	17.	Here I Go Again	Whitesnake
6/13	1	1	18.	Always	Atlantic Starr
6/20	1	1	19.	Head To Toe	Lisa Lisa & Cult Jam
8/01	1	1	20.	Shakedown	Bob Seger
12/05	1	1	21.	Heaven Is A Place On Earth	Belinda Carlisle
11/28	1	1	22.	(I've Had) The Time Of My Life	Bill Medley & Jennifer Warnes
2/07	1	1	23.	Open Your Heart	Madonna
6/06	1	1	24.	You Keep Me Hangin' On	Kim Wilde
10/17	1	1	25.	Lost In Emotion	Lisa Lisa & Cult Jam
11/21	1	1	26.	Mony Mony "Live"	Billy Idol
3/14	1	1	27.	Jacob's Ladder	Huey Lewis & The News
8/22	1	1	28.	Who's That Girl	Madonna
9/19	1	1	29.	I Just Can't Stop Loving You	Michael Jackson/Siedah Garrett
5/02	4	2	30.	Looking For A New Love	Jody Watley
10/24	3	2	31.	Causing A Commotion	Madonna
1/17	2	2	32.	C'est La Vie	Robbie Nevil
4/25	1	2	33.	Don't Dream It's Over	Crowded House
12/19	1	2	34.	Is This Love	Whitesnake
8/08	1	2	35.	I Want Your Sex	George Michael
10/17	1	2	36.	U Got The Look	Prince
1/10	1	2	37.	Notorious	Duran Duran
2/21	1	2	38.	Keep Your Hands To Yourself	Georgia Satellites
3/14	1	2	39.	Somewhere Out There	Linda Ronstadt & James Ingram
3/21	1	2	40.	Let's Wait Awhile	Janet Jackson

TOP 40 HITS
1988

PK DATE	PK WKS	PK POS	RANK	TITLE	ARTIST
7/30	4	1	1.	Roll With It	Steve Winwood
12/24	3	1	2.	Every Rose Has Its Thorn	Poison
5/28	3	1	3.	One More Try	George Michael
12/10	2	1	4.	Look Away	Chicago
3/12	2	1	5.	Never Gonna Give You Up	Rick Astley
9/10	2	1	6.	Sweet Child O' Mine	Guns N' Roses
5/14	2	1	7.	Anything For You	Gloria Estefan & Miami Sound Machine
4/09	2	1	8.	Get Outta My Dreams, Get Into My Car	Billy Ocean
3/26	2	1	9.	Man In The Mirror	Michael Jackson
7/09	2	1	10.	The Flame	Cheap Trick
2/06	2	1	11.	Could've Been	Tiffany
9/24	2	1	12.	Don't Worry Be Happy	Bobby McFerrin
10/22	2	1	13.	Groovy Kind Of Love	Phil Collins
4/23	2	1	14.	Where Do Broken Hearts Go	Whitney Houston
2/27	2	1	15.	Father Figure	George Michael
11/19	2	1	16.	Bad Medicine	Bon Jovi
8/27	2	1	17.	Monkey	George Michael
1/30	1	1	18.	Need You Tonight	INXS
1/16	1	1	19.	Got My Mind Set On You	George Harrison
1/09	1	1	20.	So Emotional	Whitney Houston
11/12	1	1	21.	Wild, Wild West	The Escape Club
2/20	1	1	22.	Seasons Change	Expose
5/07	1	1	23.	Wishing Well	Terence Trent D'Arby
12/03	1	1	24.	Baby, I Love Your Way/Freebird Medley (Free Baby)	Will To Power
7/23	1	1	25.	Hold On To The Nights	Richard Marx
6/25	1	1	26.	Foolish Beat	Debbie Gibson
10/08	1	1	27.	Love Bites	Def Leppard
1/23	1	1	28.	The Way You Make Me Feel	Michael Jackson
10/15	1	1	29.	Red Red Wine	UB40
6/18	1	1	30.	Together Forever	Rick Astley
11/05	1	1	31.	Kokomo	The Beach Boys
7/02	1	1	32.	Dirty Diana	Michael Jackson
5/14	3	2	33.	Shattered Dreams	Johnny Hates Jazz
8/06	2	2	34.	Hands To Heaven	Breathe
3/26	2	2	35.	Endless Summer Nights	Richard Marx
9/10	2	2	36.	Simply Irresistible	Robert Palmer
2/20	2	2	37.	What Have I Done To Deserve This?	Pet Shop Boys/Dusty Springfield
4/16	2	2	38.	Devil Inside	INXS
7/09	2	2	39.	Mercedes Boy	Pebbles
7/23	1	2	40.	Pour Some Sugar On Me	Def Leppard

TOP 40 HITS
1989

PK DATE	PK WKS	PK POS	RANK	TITLE	ARTIST
12/23	4	1	1.	Another Day In Paradise	Phil Collins
10/07	4	1	2.	Miss You Much	Janet Jackson
2/11	3	1	3.	Straight Up	Paula Abdul
8/12	3	1	4.	Right Here Waiting	Richard Marx
3/04	3	1	5.	Lost In Your Eyes	Debbie Gibson
4/22	3	1	6.	Like A Prayer	Madonna
12/09	2	1	7.	We Didn't Start The Fire	Billy Joel
1/21	2	1	8.	Two Hearts	Phil Collins
11/11	2	1	9.	When I See You Smile	Bad English
11/25	2	1	10.	Blame It On The Rain	Milli Vanilli
5/20	2	1	11.	Forever Your Girl	Paula Abdul
9/23	2	1	12.	Girl I'm Gonna Miss You	Milli Vanilli
7/22	2	1	13.	Toy Soldiers	Martika
9/02	1	1	14.	Cold Hearted	Paula Abdul
9/16	1	1	15.	Don't Wanna Lose You	Gloria Estefan
6/10	1	1	16.	Wind Beneath My Wings	Bette Midler
1/14	1	1	17.	My Prerogative	Bobby Brown
4/15	1	1	18.	She Drives Me Crazy	Fine Young Cannibals
4/08	1	1	19.	The Look	Roxette
7/15	1	1	20.	If You Don't Know Me By Now	Simply Red
11/04	1	1	21.	Listen To Your Heart	Roxette
6/17	1	1	22.	I'll Be Loving You (Forever)	New Kids On The Block
7/01	1	1	23.	Baby Don't Forget My Number	Milli Vanilli
3/25	1	1	24.	The Living Years	Mike & The Mechanics
4/01	1	1	25.	Eternal Flame	Bangles
5/13	1	1	26.	I'll Be There For You	Bon Jovi
7/08	1	1	27.	Good Thing	Fine Young Cannibals
9/09	1	1	28.	Hangin' Tough	New Kids On The Block
8/05	1	1	29.	Batdance	Prince
2/04	1	1	30.	When I'm With You	Sheriff
6/03	1	1	31.	Rock On	Michael Damian
6/24	1	1	32.	Satisfied	Richard Marx
8/05	3	2	33.	On Our Own	Bobby Brown
12/23	2	2	34.	Don't Know Much	Linda Ronstadt feat. Aaron Neville
9/23	2	2	35.	Heaven	Warrant
5/20	2	2	36.	Real Love	Jody Watley
10/07	2	2	37.	Cherish	Madonna
7/15	2	2	38.	Express Yourself	Madonna
1/21	1	2	39.	Don't Rush Me	Taylor Dayne
4/01	1	2	40.	Girl You Know It's True	Milli Vanilli

TOP 40 HITS
1990

PK DATE	PK WKS	PK POS	RANK	TITLE	ARTIST
12/08	4	1	1.	Because I Love You (The Postman Song)	Stevie B
4/21	4	1	2.	Nothing Compares 2 U	Sinead O'Connor
8/04	4	1	3.	Vision Of Love	Mariah Carey
5/19	3	1	4.	Vogue	Madonna
3/03	3	1	5.	Escapade	Janet Jackson
11/10	3	1	6.	Love Takes Time	Mariah Carey
2/10	3	1	7.	Opposites Attract	Paula Abdul with The Wild Pair
6/30	3	1	8.	Step By Step	New Kids On The Block
1/20	3	1	9.	How Am I Supposed To Live Without You	Michael Bolton
6/16	2	1	10.	It Must Have Been Love	Roxette
3/24	2	1	11.	Black Velvet	Alannah Myles
9/15	2	1	12.	Release Me	Wilson Phillips
7/21	2	1	13.	She Ain't Worth It	Glenn Medeiros (Feat. Bobby Brown)
6/09	1	1	14.	Hold On	Wilson Phillips
9/08	1	1	15.	Blaze Of Glory	Jon Bon Jovi
12/01	1	1	16.	I'm Your Baby Tonight	Whitney Houston
10/06	1	1	17.	Close To You	Maxi Priest
10/20	1	1	18.	I Don't Have The Heart	James Ingram
11/03	1	1	19.	Ice Ice Baby	Vanilla Ice
9/29	1	1	20.	(Can't Live Without Your) Love And Affection	Nelson
9/01	1	1	21.	If Wishes Came True	Sweet Sensation
4/07	1	1	22.	Love Will Lead You Back	Taylor Dayne
10/13	1	1	23.	Praying For Time	George Michael
4/14	1	1	24.	I'll Be Your Everything	Tommy Page
10/27	1	1	25.	Black Cat	Janet Jackson
4/14	3	2	26.	Don't Wanna Fall In Love	Jane Child
1/20	2	2	27.	Pump Up The Jam	Technotronic feat. Felly
5/26	2	2	28.	All I Wanna Do Is Make Love To You	Heart
2/10	2	2	29.	Two To Make It Right	Seduction
1/06	2	2	30.	Rhythm Nation	Janet Jackson
3/03	2	2	31.	Dangerous	Roxette
8/18	2	2	32.	Come Back To Me	Janet Jackson
11/10	2	2	33.	Pray	M.C. Hammer
12/15	1	2	34.	From A Distance	Bette Midler
8/04	1	2	35.	Cradle Of Love	Billy Idol
7/21	1	2	36.	Hold On	En Vogue
8/11	1	2	37.	The Power	Snap!
5/05	1	2	38.	I Wanna Be Rich	Calloway
11/24	1	2	39.	More Than Words Can Say	Alias
6/09	4	3	40.	Poison	Bell Biv DeVoe

TOP 40 HITS
1991

PK DATE	PK WKS	PK POS	RANK	TITLE	ARTIST
7/27	7	1	1.	(Everything I Do) I Do It For You	Bryan Adams
12/07	7	1	2.	Black Or White	Michael Jackson
6/15	5	1	3.	Rush, Rush	Paula Abdul
10/12	3	1	4.	Emotions	Mariah Carey
2/09	2	1	5.	Gonna Make You Sweat (Everybody Dance Now)	C & C Music Factory
1/26	2	1	6.	The First Time	Surface
5/25	2	1	7.	I Don't Wanna Cry	Mariah Carey
1/05	2	1	8.	Justify My Love	Madonna
4/27	2	1	9.	Baby Baby..	Amy Grant
11/09	2	1	10.	Cream	Prince & The N.P.G.
2/23	2	1	11.	All The Man That I Need	Whitney Houston
3/09	2	1	12.	Someday	Mariah Carey
9/21	2	1	13.	I Adore Mi Amor....................................	Color Me Badd
3/30	2	1	14.	Coming Out Of The Dark	Gloria Estefan
6/08	1	1	15.	More Than Words	Extreme
5/18	1	1	16.	I Like The Way (The Kissing Game)	Hi-Five
3/23	1	1	17.	One More Try	Timmy -T-
7/20	1	1	18.	Unbelievable	EMF
11/23	1	1	19.	When A Man Loves A Woman	Michael Bolton
11/30	1	1	20.	Set Adrift On Memory Bliss.....................	PM Dawn
11/02	1	1	21.	Romantic	Karyn White
1/19	1	1	22.	Love Will Never Do (Without You).............	Janet Jackson
10/05	1	1	23.	Good Vibrations	Marky Mark & The Funky Bunch
4/20	1	1	24.	You're In Love	Wilson Phillips
4/13	1	1	25.	I've Been Thinking About You...................	Londonbeat
5/11	1	1	26.	Joyride...	Roxette
9/14	1	1	27.	The Promise Of A New Day	Paula Abdul
12/14	4	2	28.	It's So Hard To Say Goodbye To Yesterday...	Boyz II Men
6/08	4	2	29.	I Wanna Sex You Up...............................	Color Me Badd
10/19	2	2	30.	Do Anything	Natural Selection
5/18	2	2	31.	Touch Me (All Night Long).......................	Cathy Dennis
8/03	2	2	32.	P.A.S.S.I.O.N.	Rythm Syndicate
7/27	1	2	33.	Right Here, Right Now............................	Jesus Jones
11/16	1	2	34.	Can't Stop This Thing We Started..............	Bryan Adams
8/17	1	2	35.	Every Heartbeat	Amy Grant
8/24	1	2	36.	It Ain't Over 'Til It's Over	Lenny Kravitz
8/31	1	2	37.	Fading Like A Flower (Every Time You Leave)..	Roxette
1/12	2	3	38.	High Enough...	Damn Yankees
9/07	2	3	39.	Motownphilly	Boyz II Men
4/13	1	3	40.	Hold You Tight......................................	Tara Kemp

TOP 40 HITS
1992

PK DATE	PK WKS	PK POS	RANK	TITLE	ARTIST
11/28	14	1	1.	I Will Always Love You	Whitney Houston
8/15	13	1	2.	End of the Road	Boyz II Men
4/25	8	1	3.	Jump	Kris Kross
7/04	5	1	4.	Baby Got Back	Sir Mix-A-Lot
3/21	5	1	5.	Save The Best For Last	Vanessa Williams
2/08	3	1	6.	I'm Too Sexy	Right Said Fred
2/29	3	1	7.	To Be With You	Mr. Big
11/14	2	1	8.	How Do You Talk To An Angel	The Heights
6/20	2	1	9.	I'll Be There	Mariah Carey
1/25	1	1	10.	All 4 Love	Color Me Badd
8/08	1	1	11.	This Used To Be My Playground	Madonna
2/01	1	1	12.	Don't Let The Sun Go Down On Me	George Michael/Elton John
11/21	8	2	13.	If I Ever Fall In Love	Shai
8/15	6	2	14.	Baby-Baby-Baby	TLC
9/26	6	2	15.	Sometimes Love Just Ain't Enough	Patty Smyth with Don Henley
3/28	4	2	16.	Tears In Heaven	Eric Clapton
12/26	3	2	17.	Rump Shaker	Wreckx-N-Effect
5/16	3	2	18.	My Lovin' (You're Never Gonna Get It)	En Vogue
2/01	3	2	19.	I Love Your Smile	Shanice
6/06	1	2	20.	Under The Bridge	Red Hot Chili Peppers
1/25	1	2	21.	Can't Let Go	Mariah Carey
5/09	1	2	22.	Bohemian Rhapsody	Queen
10/31	4	3	23.	I'd Die Without You	PM Dawn
3/07	4	3	24.	Remember The Time	Michael Jackson
9/12	3	3	25.	Humpin' Around	Bobby Brown
10/10	2	3	26.	Jump Around	House Of Pain
8/29	2	3	27.	November Rain	Guns N' Roses
4/11	1	3	28.	Masterpiece	Atlantic Starr
2/15	1	3	29.	Diamonds And Pearls	Prince & The N.P.G.
10/24	1	3	30.	Erotica	Madonna
7/18	3	4	31.	Achy Breaky Heart	Billy Ray Cyrus
5/23	2	4	32.	Live And Learn	Joe Public
7/11	1	4	33.	If You Asked Me To	Celine Dion
9/19	1	4	34.	Stay	Shakespear's Sister
1/18	2	5	35.	Finally	Ce Ce Peniston
6/27	2	5	36.	Damn I Wish I Was Your Lover	Sophie B. Hawkins
8/01	1	5	37.	Just Another Day	Jon Secada
10/17	1	5	38.	She's Playing Hard To Get	Hi-Five
4/11	1	5	39.	Make It Happen	Mariah Carey
1/11	1	5	40.	2 Legit 2 Quit	Hammer

THE
TOP 100
ALBUMS

This section displays, in rank order, the biggest No. 1 albums fro January, 1955 through March, 1993.

This ranking is based on the most weeks an album held the No. 1 positic Ties are broken according to this order: total weeks in the Top 10, to weeks in the Top 40, and finally, total weeks charted. The total weeks at N 1 and total weeks in the Top 10 are shown below each album cover pho along with the year the album peaked.

(Whitney Houston's album "The Bodyguard" was still in the Top 10 as the April 10, 1993 cutoff date.)

1. **"West Side Story"**
Soundtrack

#1 – 54 Weeks
Top 10 Weeks: 106
Year: 1962

2. **"Thriller"**
Michael Jackson

#1 – 37 Weeks
Top 10 Weeks: 78
Year: 1983

3. **"South Pacific"**
Soundtrack

#1 – 31 Weeks
Top 10 Weeks: 90
Year: 1958

4. **"Calypso"**
Harry Belafonte

#1 – 31 Weeks
Top 10 Weeks: 58
Year: 1956

5. **"Rumours"**
Fleetwood Mac

#1 – 31 Weeks
Top 10 Weeks: 52
Year: 1977

6. **"Saturday Night Fever"**
Bee Gees/Soundtrack

#1 – 24 Weeks
Top 10 Weeks: 35
Year: 1978

7. **"Purple Rain"**
Prince And The
Revolution/Soundtrack

#1 – 24 Weeks
Top 10 Weeks: 32
Year: 1984

8.
"Please Hammer Don't Hurt 'Em"
M.C. Hammer

#1 – 21 Weeks
Top 10 Weeks: 52
Year: 1990

9.
"Blue Hawaii"
Elvis Presley/
Soundtrack

#1 – 20 Weeks
Top 10 Weeks: 39
Year: 1961

10.
"Ropin' The Wind"
Garth Brooks

#1 – 18 Weeks
Top 10 Weeks: 50
Year: 1991

11.
"Dirty Dancing"
Soundtrack

#1 – 18 Weeks
Top 10 Weeks: 48
Year: 1987

12.
"More Of The Monkees"
The Monkees

#1 – 18 Weeks
Top 10 Weeks: 25
Year: 1967

13.
"Some Gave All"
Billy Ray Cyrus

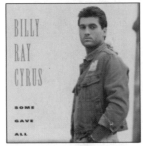

#1 – 17 Weeks
Top 10 Weeks: 43
Year: 1992

14.
"Synchronicity"
The Police

#1 – 17 Weeks
Top 10 Weeks: 40
Year: 1983

15. **"Love Me Or Leave Me"**
Doris Day/
Soundtrack

#1 – 17 Weeks
Top 10 Weeks: 25
Year: 1955

16. **"The Sound Of Music"**
Original Cast

#1 – 16 Weeks
Top 10 Weeks: 105
Year: 1960

"To The Extreme"
Vanilla Ice

#1 – 16 Weeks
Top 10 Weeks: 26
Year: 1990

18. **"Days of Wine And Roses"**
Andy Williams

#1 – 16 Weeks
Top 10 Weeks: 23
Year: 1963

19. **"My Fair Lady"**
Original Cast

#1 – 15 Weeks
Top 10 Weeks: 173
Year: 1956

20. **"Tapestry"**
Carole King

#1 – 15 Weeks
Top 10 Weeks: 46
Year: 1971

21. **"Sgt. Pepper's Lonely Hearts Club Band"**
The Beatles

#1 – 15 Weeks
Top 10 Weeks: 33
Year: 1967

22. **"Business As Usual"**
Men At Work

#1 – 15 Weeks
Top 10 Weeks: 31
Year: 1982

23. **"The Kingston Trio At Large"**
The Kingston Trio

#1 – 15 Weeks
Top 10 Weeks: 31
Year: 1959

24. **"Hi Infidelity"**
REO Speedwagon

#1 – 15 Weeks
Top 10 Weeks: 30
Year: 1981

25. **"The Wall"**
Pink Floyd

#1 – 15 Weeks
Top 10 Weeks: 27
Year: 1980

26. **"Mary Poppins"**
Soundtrack

#1 – 14 Weeks
Top 10 Weeks: 48
Year: 1965

27. **"Whitney Houston"**
Whitney Houston

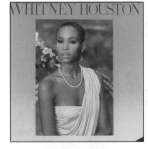

#1 – 14 Weeks
Top 10 Weeks: 46
Year: 1986

28. **"The Button-Down Mind Of Bob Newhart"**
Bob Newhart

#1 – 14 Weeks
Top 10 Weeks: 44
Year: 1960

29. **"Exodus"**
Soundtrack

#1 – 14 Weeks
Top 10 Weeks: 38
Year: 1961

30. **"Songs In The Key Of Life"**
Stevie Wonder

#1 – 14 Weeks
Top 10 Weeks: 35
Year: 1976

"Modern Sounds In Country And Western Music"
Ray Charles

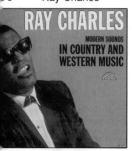

#1 – 14 Weeks
Top 10 Weeks: 33
Year: 1962

32. **"A Hard Day's Night"**
The Beatles/Soundtrack

#1 – 14 Weeks
Top 10 Weeks: 28
Year: 1964

33. **"The Bodyguard"***
Whitney Houston/
Soundtrack

#1 – 14 Weeks
Top 10 Weeks: 19↟
Year: 1992
*Still in Top 10 as of
April 10, 1993 cutoff date

34. **"Persuasive Percussion"**
Enoch Light/
Terry Snyder and The
All-Stars

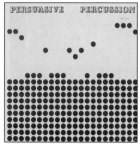

#1 – 13 Weeks
Top 10 Weeks: 43
Year: 1960

35. **"Judy At Carnegie Hall"**
Judy Garland

#1 – 13 Weeks
Top 10 Weeks: 37
Year: 1961

36. **"The Monkees"**
The Monkees

#1 – 13 Weeks
Top 10 Weeks: 32
Year: 1966

37. **"Hair"**
Original Cast

#1 – 13 Weeks
Top 10 Weeks: 28
Year: 1969

38. **"The Music Man"**
Original Cast

#1 – 12 Weeks
Top 10 Weeks: 66
Year: 1958

39. **"Faith"**
George Michael

#1 – 12 Weeks
Top 10 Weeks: 51
Year: 1988

40. **"Breakfast At Tiffany's"**
Henry Mancini/
Soundtrack

#1 – 12 Weeks
Top 10 Weeks: 46
Year: 1962

41. **"Sold Out"**
The Kingston Trio

#1 – 12 Weeks
Top 10 Weeks: 29
Year: 1960

42. **"Grease"**
Soundtrack

#1 – 12 Weeks
Top 10 Weeks: 29
Year: 1978

43. **"The First Family"**
Vaughn Meader

#1 – 12 Weeks
Top 10 Weeks: 17
Year: 1962

44. **"Mariah Carey"**
Mariah Carey

#1 – 11 Weeks
Top 10 Weeks: 49
Year: 1991

"Calcutta!"
Lawrence Welk

#1 – 11 Weeks
Top 10 Weeks: 33
Year: 1961

46. **"Whitney"**
Whitney Houston

#1 – 11 Weeks
Top 10 Weeks: 31
Year: 1987

47. **"Abbey Road"**
The Beatles

#1 – 11 Weeks
Top 10 Weeks: 27
Year: 1969

48. **"Meet The
Beatles!"**
The Beatles

#1 – 11 Weeks
Top 10 Weeks: 21
Year: 1964

49. **"Miami Vice"**
TV Soundtrack

#1 – 11 Weeks
Top 10 Weeks: 18
Year: 1985

50. **"Forever Your Girl"**
Paula Abdul

#1 – 10 Weeks
Top 10 Weeks: 64
Year: 1989

51. **"Around The World In 80 Days"**
Soundtrack

#1 – 10 Weeks
Top 10 Weeks: 54
Year: 1957

52. **"Gigi"**
Soundtrack

#1 – 10 Weeks
Top 10 Weeks: 54
Year: 1958

53. **"Frampton Comes Alive!"**
Peter Frampton

#1 – 10 Weeks
Top 10 Weeks: 52
Year: 1976

54. **"Elvis Presley"**
Elvis Presley

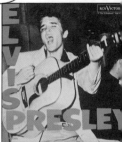

#1 – 10 Weeks
Top 10 Weeks: 43
Year: 1956

55. **"The Music From Peter Gunn"**
Henry Mancini

#1 – 10 Weeks
Top 10 Weeks: 43
Year: 1959

56. **"4"**
Foreigner

#1 – 10 Weeks
Top 10 Weeks: 34
Year: 1981

57. **"G.I. Blues"**
Elvis Presley/
Soundtrack

#1 – 10 Weeks
Top 10 Weeks: 29
Year: 1960

58. **"Footloose"**
Soundtrack

#1 – 10 Weeks
Top 10 Weeks: 20
Year: 1984

"String Along"
The Kingston Trio

#1 – 10 Weeks
Top 10 Weeks: 20
Year: 1960

60. **"Loving You"**
Elvis Presley/
Soundtrack

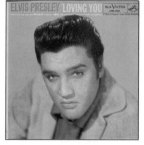

#1 – 10 Weeks
Top 10 Weeks: 19
Year: 1957

61. **"The Singing Nun"**
The Singing Nun

#1 – 10 Weeks
Top 10 Weeks: 18
Year: 1963

62. **"Bridge Over
Troubled Water"**
Simon and Garfunkel

#1 – 10 Weeks
Top 10 Weeks: 17
Year: 1970

63. **"Elton John –
Greatest Hits"**
Elton John

#1 – 10 Weeks
Top 10 Weeks: 11
Year: 1974

64. **"Brothers In Arms"**
Dire Straits

#1 – 9 Weeks
Top 10 Weeks: 37
Year: 1985

65. **"The Joshua Tree"**
U2

#1 – 9 Weeks
Top 10 Weeks: 35
Year: 1987

66. **"What Now My Love"**
Herb Alpert & the Tijuana Brass

#1 – 9 Weeks
Top 10 Weeks: 32
Year: 1966

67. **"Asia"**
Asia

#1 – 9 Weeks
Top 10 Weeks: 27
Year: 1982

68. **"The Graduate"**
Simon & Garfunkel
Soundtrack

#1 – 9 Weeks
Top 10 Weeks: 26
Year: 1968

69. **"American Fool"**
John Cougar

#1 – 9 Weeks
Top 10 Weeks: 22
Year: 1982

70. **"Tattoo You"**
The Rolling Stones

#1 – 9 Weeks
Top 10 Weeks: 22
Year: 1981

71. **"Stars For A Summer Night"**
Various Artists

#1 – 9 Weeks
Top 10 Weeks: 21
Year: 1961

72. **"The Long Run"**
Eagles

#1 – 9 Weeks
Top 10 Weeks: 21
Year: 1979

"Nice 'n' Easy"
Frank Sinatra

#1 – 9 Weeks
Top 10 Weeks: 19
Year: 1960

74. **"Cosmo's Factory"**
Creedence Clearwater
Revival

#1 – 9 Weeks
Top 10 Weeks: 19
Year: 1970

75. **"Beatle's 65"**
The Beatles

#1 – 9 Weeks
Top 10 Weeks: 16
Year: 1965

76. **"Help!"**
The Beatles/
Soundtrack

#1 – 9 Weeks
Top 10 Weeks: 15
Year: 1965

77. **"The Beatles
[White Album]"**
The Beatles

#1 – 9 Weeks
Top 10 Weeks: 15
Year: 1968

78. **"Pearl"**
Janis Joplin

#1 – 9 Weeks
Top 10 Weeks: 15
Year: 1971

79. **"Chicago V"**
Chicago

#1 – 9 Weeks
Top 10 Weeks: 13
Year: 1972

80. **"Whipped Cream & Other Delights"**
Herb Alpert's Tijuana Brass

#1 – 8 Weeks
Top 10 Weeks: 61
Year: 1965

81. **"Sing Along With Mitch"**
Mitch Miller & The Gang

#1 – 8 Weeks
Top 10 Weeks: 53
Year: 1958

82. **"Slippery When Wet"**
Bon Jovi

#1 – 8 Weeks
Top 10 Weeks: 46
Year: 1986

83. **"Girl You Know It's True"**
Milli Vanilli

#1 – 8 Weeks
Top 10 Weeks: 41
Year: 1989

84. **"Goodbye Yellow Brick Road"**
Elton John

#1 – 8 Weeks
Top 10 Weeks: 36
Year: 1973

85. **"Love Is The Thing"**
Nat "King" Cole

#1 – 8 Weeks
Top 10 Weeks: 31
Year: 1957

86. **"Hotel California"**
Eagles

#1 – 8 Weeks
Top 10 Weeks: 28
Year: 1977

"Here We Go Again!"
The Kingston Trio

#1 – 8 Weeks
Top 10 Weeks: 26
Year: 1959

88. **"Double Fantasy"**
John Lennon/
Yoko Ono

#1 – 8 Weeks
Top 10 Weeks: 24
Year: 1980

89. **"52nd Street"**
Billy Joel

#1 – 8 Weeks
Top 10 Weeks: 22
Year: 1978

"Cheap Thrills"
Big Brother And the
Holding Company

#1 – 8 Weeks
Top 10 Weeks: 19
Year: 1968

91. **"Magical Mystery Tour"**
The Beatles

#1 – 8 Weeks
Top 10 Weeks: 14
Year: 1968

92. **"My Son, The Nut"**
Allan Sherman

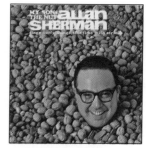

#1 – 8 Weeks
Top 10 Weeks: 12
Year: 1963

93. **"Peter, Paul and Mary"**
Peter, Paul and Mary

#1 – 7 Weeks
Top 10 Weeks: 85
Year: 1962

94. **"Born In The U.S.A."**
Bruce Springsteen

#1 – 7 Weeks
Top 10 Weeks: 84
Year: 1984

95. **"Blood, Sweat & Tears"**
Blood, Sweat & Tears

#1 – 7 Weeks
Top 10 Weeks: 50
Year: 1969

96. **"Stereo 35/MM"**
Enoch Light & The Light Brigade

#1 – 7 Weeks
Top 10 Weeks: 42
Year: 1961

97. **"Tchaikovsky: Piano Concerto N**
Van Cliburn

#1 – 7 Weeks
Top 10 Weeks: 39
Year: 1958

98. **"No Jacket Required"**
Phil Collins

#1 – 7 Weeks
Top 10 Weeks: 31
Year: 1985

99. **"The Raw & The Cooked"**
Fine Young Cannibals

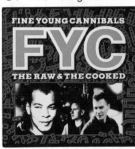

#1 – 7 Weeks
Top 10 Weeks: 27
Year: 1989

100. **"Led Zeppelin I**
Led Zeppelin

#1 – 7 Weeks
Top 10 Weeks: 24
Year: 1969

APPLE
1815

BAD*f*INGER

FROM THE SOUNDTRACK OF THE FILM 'THE MAGIC CHRISTIAN'

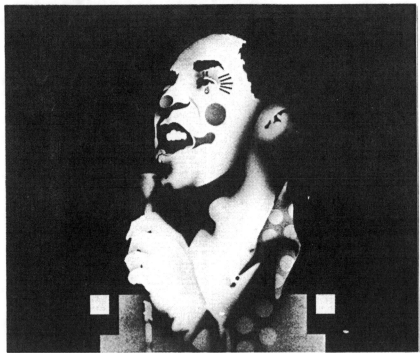

THE ARTISTS

This section lists, alphabetically by artist name, every single listed in the *Top 1000* ranking.

Each artist's hits are listed in rank order, showing the *Top 1000* ranking next to each title, along the original label and number. Because the artist's hits are listed in rank order, it makes for a handy guide to easily see each artist's all-time greatest hits.

A

ABBA
601 Dancing Queen ....Atlantic 3372
ABBOTT, Gregory
596 Shake You Down ....Columbia 06191
ABDUL, Paula
87 Rush, Rush ....Virgin 98828
258 Straight Up ....Virgin 99256
262 Opposites Attract...................Virgin 99158
Paula Abdul With The Wild Pair
468 Forever Your Girl ....Virgin 99230
604 Cold Hearted ....Virgin 99196
810 The Promise Of A New Day ....Virgin 98752
ADAMS, Bryan
33 (Everything I Do) I Do It For
You ....A&M 1567
476 Heaven ....A&M 2729
A-HA
642 Take On Me ....Warner 29011
AIR SUPPLY
620 The One That You Love ....Arista 0604
854 All Out Of Love ....Arista 0520
893 Making Love Out Of Nothing At
All...............................Arista 9056
ALPERT, Herb, & The Tijuana Brass
162 This Guy's In Love With You ......A&M 929
341 Rise ....A&M 2151
AMERICA
207 A Horse With No Name ....Warner 7555
829 Sister Golden Hair ....Warner 8086
ANDERSON, Carl - see LORING, Gloria
ANGELS, The
223 My Boyfriend's Back ....Smash 1834
ANIMALS, The
255 The House Of The Rising Sun ...MGM 13264
ANKA, Paul
129 Lonely Boy ....ABC-Para. 10022
291 (You're) Having My Baby.....United Art. 454
526 Diana ....ABC-Para. 9831
885 Put Your Head On My
Shoulder....................ABC-Para. 10040
ARCHIES, The
110 Sugar, Sugar ....Calendar 1008
ARMSTRONG, Louis
522 Hello, Dolly! ....Kapp 573
ASSOCIATION, The
145 Windy..............................Warner 7041
289 Cherish.............................Valiant 747
986 Never My Love....................Warner 7074
ASTLEY, Rick
424 Never Gonna Give You Up ....RCA 5347
776 Together Forever ....RCA 8319
ATLANTIC STARR
658 Always ....Warner 28455
AUSTIN, Patti, with James Ingram
327 Baby, Come To Me.............Qwest 50036
AVALON, Frankie
81 Venus ....Chancellor 1031

586 Why ....Chancellor 1045
AWB (Average White Band)
687 Pick Up The Pieces..............Atlantic 3229

B

BACHMAN-TURNER OVERDRIVE
812 You Ain't Seen Nothing Yet ..Mercury 73622
BAD ENGLISH
464 When I See You Smile ....Epic 69082
BAILEY, Philip, with Phil Collins
991 Easy Lover ....Columbia 04679
BANANARAMA
693 Venus ....London 886056
BANGLES
154 Walk Like An Egyptian ....Columbia 06257
751 Eternal Flame..................Columbia 68533
BASIL, Toni
538 Mickey ....Chrysalis 2638
BAXTER, Les
37 The Poor People Of Paris........Capitol 3336
BAY CITY ROLLERS
777 Saturday Night ....Arista 0149
BEACH BOYS, The
354 I Get Around.....................Capitol 5174
449 Help Me, Rhonda ....Capitol 5395
705 Good Vibrations ....Capitol 5676
800 Kokomo ....Elektra 69385
BEATLES, The
10 Hey Jude..~.....................Apple 2276
29 I Want To Hold Your Hand .....Capitol 5112
93 Get Back.~.......................Apple 2490
96 Can't Buy Me Love ....Capitol 5150
169 Yesterday.~......................Capitol 5498
254 Hello Goodbye ....Capitol 2056
281 We Can Work It Out ....Capitol 5555
283 I Feel Fine ....Capitol 5327
290 Help! ....Capitol 5476
312 She Loves You ....Swan 4152
313 Let It Be ~......................Apple 2764
407 A Hard Day's Night ....Capitol 5222
506 The Long And Winding Road ~.Apple 2832
514 Paperback Writer ....Capitol 5651
515 Eight Days A Week ....Capitol 5371
569 Come Together ~.................Apple 2654
725 All You Need Is Love.............Capitol 5964
790 Love Me Do ~....................Tollie 9008
798 Ticket To Ride ....Capitol 5407
825 Penny Lane.~....................Capitol 5810
866 Twist And Shout...................Tollie 9001
BEE GEES
19 Night Fever ....RSO 889
103 Stayin' Alive ....RSO 885
130 How Can You Mend A Broken
Heart..............................Atco 6824
172 How Deep Is Your Love ....RSO 882
337 Too Much Heaven ....RSO 913
348 Tragedy ....RSO 918
402 Jive Talkin' ....RSO 510

CROSS, Christopher
181 Arthur's Theme (Best That You Can Do) ....Warner 49787
677 Sailing ....Warner 49507
858 Ride Like The Wind ....Warner 49184
CRYSTALS, The
441 He's A Rebel ....Philles 106
CULTURE CLUB
211 Karma Chameleon ....Virgin 04221
892 Do You Really Want To Hurt Me ....Epic 03368
960 Time (Clock Of The Heart)........Epic 03796
CUTTING CREW
485 (I Just) Died In Your Arms......Virgin 99481

D

DALE & GRACE
445 I'm Leaving It Up To You........Montel 921
DAMIAN, Michael
806 Rock On ....Cypress 1420
DANNY & THE JUNIORS
25 At The Hop ....ABC-Para. 9871
D'ARBY, Terence Trent
731 Wishing Well ....Columbia 07675
DARIN, Bobby
7 Mack The Knife......................Atco 6147
DAVIS, Mac
217 Baby Don't Get Hooked On Me ....Columbia 45618
DAVIS, Sammy Jr.
259 The Candy Man...................MGM 14320
DAWN
115 Tie A Yellow Ribbon Round The Ole Oak Tree ....Bell 45318
190 Knock Three Times...................Bell 938
292 He Don't Love You (Like I Love You)..........................Elektra 45240
Tony Orlando & Dawn
DAY, Bobby
946 Rock-in Robin........................Class 229
DAY, Doris
875 Whatever Will Be, Will Be (Que Sera, Sera) ....Columbia 40704
DAYNE, Taylor
737 Love Will Lead You Back........Arista 9938
DEAN, Jimmy
84 Big Bad John ....Columbia 42175
DEE, Joey, & the Starliters
191 Peppermint Twist - Part I ......Roulette 4401
DEE, Kiki - see JOHN, Elton
DEES, Rick, and His Cast Of Idiots
540 Disco Duck (Part 1) ....RSO 857
DEF LEPPARD
754 Love Bites....................Mercury 870402
DENVER, John
448 Annie's Song ....RCA 0295
683 Sunshine On My Shoulders ....RCA 0213
801 Thank God I'm A Country Boy ..RCA 10239

827 I'm Sorry ....RCA 10353
871 Calypso ....RCA 10353
DeSARIO, Teri, with K.C.
992 Yes, I'm Ready ....Casablanca 2227
DEXYS MIDNIGHT RUNNERS
739 Come On Eileen.................Mercury 76189
DIAMOND, Neil
321 You Don't Bring Me Flowers......................Columbia 10840
Barbra Streisand & Neil Diamond
673 Cracklin' Rosie......................Uni 55250
786 Song Sung Blue..................Uni 55326
888 Love On The Rocks.............Capitol 4939
DIAMONDS, The
835 Little Darlin' ....Mercury 71060
DINNING, Mark
322 Teen Angel ....MGM 12845
DION
364 Runaround Sue ....Laurie 3110
932 Ruby Baby ....Columbia 42662
DIRE STRAITS
237 Money For Nothing ....Warner 28950
DIXIE CUPS, The
280 Chapel Of Love....................Red Bird 001
DOGGETT, Bill
872 Honky Tonk (Parts 1 & 2)........King 4950
DOMINO, Fats
873 Blueberry Hill ....Imperial 5407
DONALDSON, Bo, And The Heywoods
440 Billy, Don't Be A Hero ....ABC 11435
DONOVAN
719 Sunshine Superman ....Epic 10045
921 Mellow Yellow ....Epic 10098
DOOBIE BROTHERS, The
579 What A Fool Believes ....Warner 8725
696 Black Water ....Warner 8062
DOORS, The
213 Light My Fire ....Elektra 45615
371 Hello, I Love You ....Elektra 45635
DORSEY, Jimmy
846 So Rare ....Fraternity 755
DOUGLAS, Carl
401 Kung Fu Fighting...........20th Century 2140
DOVELLS, The
959 Bristol Stomp ....Parkway 827
DOWELL, Joe
698 Wooden Heart ....Smash 1708
DRIFTERS, The
214 Save The Last Dance For Me...Atlantic 2071
DURAN DURAN
382 The Reflex........................Capitol 5345
487 A View To A Kill................Capitol 5475
864 The Wild Boys ....Capitol 5417

E

EAGLES
546 One Of These Nights ....Asylum 45257
584 Heartache Tonight ....Asylum 46545

HEYWOOD, Eddie - see WINTERHALTER, Hugo

HI-FIVE
558 I Like The Way (The Kissing Game) ....Jive 1424

HIGHWAYMEN, The
369 Michael............................United Art. 258

HOLLIES, The
980 Long Cool Woman (In A Black Dress) ....Epic 10871

HOLLOWAY, Loletta - see MARKY MARK

HOLLY, Buddy - see CRICKETS, The

HOLLYWOOD ARGYLES
629 Alley-Oop ....Lute 5905

HOLMES, Clint
967 Playground In My Mind ....Epic 10891

HOLMES, Rupert
198 Escape (The Pina Colada Song) ....Infinity 50035

HONEY CONE, The
625 Want Ads........................Hot Wax 7011

HOPKIN, Mary
913 Those Were The Days ....Apple 1801

HORNSBY, Bruce, & The Range
602 The Way It Is ....RCA 5023

HORTON, Johnny
46 The Battle Of New Orleans ..Columbia 41339

HOUSTON, Thelma
594 Don't Leave Me This Way ......Tamla 54278

HOUSTON, Whitney
1 I Will Always Love You ....Arista 12490
265 Greatest Love Of All ....Arista 9466
346 I Wanna Dance With Somebody (Who Loves Me).........................Arista 9598
420 All The Man That I Need ....Arista 2156
439 Didn't We Almost Have It All ...Arista 9616
462 How Will I Know ....Arista 9434
486 Where Do Broken Hearts Go ....Arista 9674
618 I'm Your Baby Tonight...........Arista 2108
619 So Emotional ....Arista 9642
647 Saving All My Love For You ....Arista 9381

HUES CORPORATION, The
817 Rock The Boat ....RCA 0232

HUMAN LEAGUE, The
179 Don't You Want Me...............A&M 2397
651 Human ....A&M 2861

HUNTER, Tab
47 Young Love ....Dot 15533

HYLAND, Brian
627 Itsy Bitsy Teenie Weenie Yellow Polkadot Bikini................................Kapp 342

I

IDOL, Billy
773 Mony Mony 'Live'.............Chrysalis 43161

INGRAM, James
327 Baby, Come To Me...............Qwest 50036
Patti Austin with James Ingram
643 I Don't Have The Heart ....Warner 19911

INXS
593 Need You Tonight ....Atlantic 89188

J

JACKS, Terry
226 Seasons In The Sun ....Bell 45432

JACKSON, Janet
157 Miss You Much ....A&M 1445
228 Escapade ....A&M 1490
484 When I Think Of You ....A&M 2855
646 Love Will Never Do (Without You) ....A&M 1538
815 Black Cat...........................A&M 1477

JACKSON, Michael
31 Billie Jean ....Epic 03509
34 Black Or White ....Epic 74100
45 Say Say Say ....Columbia 04168
Paul McCartney & Michael Jackson
135 Rock With You......................Epic 50797
194 Beat It ....Epic 03759
438 Man In The Mirror ....Epic 07668
511 Bad ....Epic 07418
710 Ben ....Motown 1207
763 The Way You Make Me Feel .....Epic 07645
774 Don't Stop 'Til You Get Enough .Epic 50742
791 I Just Can't Stop Loving You .....Epic 07253
816 Dirty Diana ....Epic 07739
891 The Girl Is Mine.....................Epic 03288
Michael Jackson/Paul McCartney
988 Rockin' Robin....................Motown 1197

JACKSON 5
72 I'll Be There......................Motown 1171
365 ABC ....Motown 1163
366 The Love You Save ....Motown 1166
567 I Want You Back..................Motown 1157
919 Never Can Say Goodbye ....Motown 1179
955 Dancing Machine.................Motown 1286

JAMES, Sonny
524 Young Love ....Capitol 3602

JAMES, Tommy, And The Shondells
309 Crimson And Clover............Roulette 7028
505 Hanky Panky ....Roulette 4686
899 Crystal Blue Persuasion........Roulette 7050

JAN & DEAN
451 Surf City..........................Liberty 55580

JEFFERSON STARSHIP - see STARSHIP

JETT, Joan, & The Blackhearts
27 I Love Rock 'N Roll............Boardwalk 135

JOEL, Billy
304 It's Still Rock And Roll To Me ....Columbia 11276
384 We Didn't Start The Fire .....Columbia 73021
653 Tell Her About It ....Columbia 04012

JOHN, Elton
155 Don't Go Breaking My Heart ..Rocket 40585
Elton John And Kiki Dee
215 Crocodile Rock ....MCA 40000
274 Island Girl.........................MCA 40461

THE SHORTEST WAY TO A HIT SINGLE IS...

JOHN ONO LENNON
INSTANT KARMA!
(WE ALL SHINE ON)

PRODUCED BY
PHIL SPECTOR

APPLE RECORDS 1818

T

TASTE OF HONEY, A
182   Boogie Oogie Oogie ....Capitol 4565
TAYLOR, James
631   You've Got A Friend ....Warner 7498
TAYLOR, Johnnie
158   Disco Lady ....Columbia 10281
TEARS FOR FEARS
268   Shout ....Mercury 880294
387   Everybody Wants To Rule The
          World.........................Mercury 880659
TECHNOTRONIC featuring FELLY
954   Pump Up The Jam................SBK 07311
TEDDY BEARS, The
186   To Know Him, Is To Love Him ....Dore 503
TEMPO, Nino, & April Stevens
703   Deep Purple ....Atco 6273
TEMPTATIONS, The
307   I Can't Get Next To You.........Gordy 7093
355   Just My Imagination (Running Away
          With Me) ....Gordy 7105
633   My Girl ....Gordy 7038
783   Papa Was A Rollin' Stone.......Gordy 7121
984   I'm Gonna Make You Love
          Me...............................Motown 1137
          Diana Ross & The Supremes & The Temptations
10cc
940   I'm Not In Love ....Mercury 73678
TEX, Joe
950   I Gotcha ....Dial 1010
THOMAS, B.J.
104   Raindrops Keep Fallin' On My
          Head........................Scepter 12265
670   (Hey Won't You Play) Another Somebody
          Done Somebody Wrong Song ..ABC 12054
THREE DEGREES, The - see MFSB
THREE DOG NIGHT
55   Joy To The World................Dunhill 4272
358   Mama Told Me (Not To
          Come).........................Dunhill 4239
824   Black & White ....Dunhill 4317
TIFFANY
473   Could've Been ....MCA 53231
481   I Think We're Alone Now........MCA 53167
TIMMY -T-
559   One More Try ....Quality 15114
TLC
837   Baby-Baby-Baby ....LaFace 24028
TOKENS, The
242   The Lion Sleeps Tonight...........RCA 7954
TORNADOES, The
240   Telstar ....London 9561
TOTO
729   Africa ....Columbia 03335
842   Rosanna ....Columbia 02811
TOYS, The
931   A Lover's Concerto ....DynoVoice 209

TRAVOLTA, John, & Olivia Newton-John
560   You're The One That I Want ....RSO 891
TROGGS, The
413   Wild Thing ....Fontana 1548
TURNER, Tina
193   What's Love Got To Do With
          It................................Capitol 5354
927   Typical Male ....Capitol 5615
TURTLES, The
(221) Happy Together ....White Whale 244
TWITTY, Conway
316   It's Only Make Believe ....MGM 12677
TYLER, Bonnie
114   Total Eclipse Of The Heart ...Columbia 03906
TYMES, The
702   So Much In Love ....Parkway 871

U

UB40
727   Red Red Wine ....A&M 1244
UNION GAP Featuring Gary Puckett
(905) Young Girl ....Columbia 44450
USA for AFRICA
160   We Are The World ....Columbia 04839
U.S. BONDS - see BONDS, Gary U.S.
U2
238   With Or Without You ....Island 99469
437   I Still Haven't Found What I'm Looking
          For ....Island 99430

V

VALENS, Ritchie
948   Donna.............................Del-Fi 4110
VALLI, Frankie
380   Grease ....RSO 897
611   My Eyes Adored You ....Private S. 45003
VANGELIS
570   Chariots Of Fire - Titles ....Polydor 2189
VAN HALEN
77   Jump.............................Warner 29384
VANILLA ICE
648   Ice Ice Baby........................SBK 07335
VEE, Bobby
278   Take Good Care Of My Baby ..Liberty 55354
VERA, Billy, & The Beaters
463   At This Moment.................Rhino 74403
VERNE, Larry
718   Mr. Custer ....Era 3024
VILLAGE PEOPLE
878   Y.M.C.A. ....Casablanca 945
VINTON, Bobby
(132) Roses Are Red (My Love) ....Epic 9509
151   There! I've Said It Again ....Epic 9638
(245) Blue Velvet ....Epic 9614
582   Mr. Lonely ....Epic 9730

W

WAITE, John
561 Missing You ....EMI America 8212
WANG CHUNG
993 Everybody Have Fun Tonight ..Geffen 28562
WARD, Anita
306 Ring My Bell ....Juana 3422
WARNES, Jennifer - see COCKER, Joe, and MEDLEY, Bill
WARRANT
995 Heaven ....Columbia 68985
WARWICK, Dionne
121 That's What Friends Are For.....Arista 9422
      Dionne & Friends
609 Then Came You ....Atlantic 3202
      Dionne Warwicke And Spinners
868 (Theme From) Valley Of The
      Dolls ....Scepter 12203
WASHINGTON, Grover Jr./Bill Withers
884 Just The Two Of Us ....Elektra 47103
WATLEY, Jody
869 Looking For A New Love ....MCA 52956
WEISSBERG, Eric, & Steve Mandell
870 Dueling Banjos ....Warner 7659
WELK, Lawrence
351 Calcutta ....Dot 16161
WELLS, Mary
398 My Guy ....Motown 1056
WHAM! - see MICHAEL, George
WHITE, Barry
831 Can't Get Enough Of Your Love,
      Babe........................20th Century 2120
WHITE, Karyn
635 Romantic........................Warner 19319
WHITESNAKE
654 Here I Go Again ....Geffen 28339
WILD CHERRY
195 Play That Funky Music ....Epic 50225
WILDE, Kim
757 You Keep Me Hangin' On ....MCA 53024
WILLIAMS, Andy
204 Butterfly ....Cadence 1308
867 Can't Get Used To Losing
      You ....Columbia 42674
WILLIAMS, Deniece
344 Let's Hear It For The Boy ....Columbia 04417
632 Too Much, Too Little, Too
      Late.........................Columbia 10693
      Johnny Mathis/Deniece Williams
WILLIAMS, Maurice, & The Zodiacs
804 Stay ....Herald 552
WILLIAMS, Roger
97 Autumn Leaves.....................Kapp 116
WILLIAMS, Vanessa
66 Save The Best For Last.........Wing 865136
WILL TO POWER
732 Baby, I Love Your Way/Freebird Medley
      (Free Baby) ....Epic 08034

WILSON, Al
640 Show And Tell ....Rocky Road 30073
WILSON, Shanice - see SHANICE
WILSON PHILLIPS
421 Release Me ....SBK 07327
554 Hold On ....SBK 07322
667 You're In Love ....SBK 07343
WINGS - see McCARTNEY, Paul
WINTER, Edgar, Group
665 Frankenstein........................Epic 10967
WINTERHALTER, Hugo/Eddie Heywood
942 Canadian Sunset....................RCA 6537
WINWOOD, Steve
165 Roll With It ....Virgin 99326
741 Higher Love......................Island 28710
WITHERS, Bill
264 Lean On Me ....Sussex 235
884 Just The Two Of Us ....Elektra 47103
      Grover Washington, Jr./Bill Withers
WONDER, Stevie
28 Ebony And Ivory..............Columbia 02860
      Paul McCartney with Stevie Wonder
200 I Just Called To Say I Love
      You..............................Motown 1745
239 Sir Duke ....Tamla 54281
275 Fingertips - Pt 2 ....Tamla 54080
610 I Wish ....Tamla 54274
615 Part-Time Lover ....Tamla 1808
666 You Haven't Done Nothin .....Tamla 54252
686 You Are The Sunshine Of My
      Life.............................Tamla 54232
767 Superstition ....Tamla 54226
987 For Once In My Life.............Tamla 54174
WOOLEY, Sheb
57 The Purple People Eater.........MGM 12651
WRECKX-N-EFFECT
874 Rump Shaker ....MCA 54388
WRIGHT, Gary
901 Dream Weaver ....Warner 8167
989 Love Is Alive ....Warner 8143

Y

YES
315 Owner Of A Lonely Heart ....Atco 99817
YOUNG, Neil
628 Heart Of Gold ....Reprise 1065
YOUNG, Paul
600 Everytime You Go Away .....Columbia 04867
YOUNG RASCALS, The
91 People Got To Be Free ....Atlantic 2537
      shown as: The Rascals
153 Groovin' ....Atlantic 2401
706 Good Lovin' ....Atlantic 2321

Z

ZAGER & EVANS
60 In The Year 2525 (Exordium &
      Terminus).........................RCA 0174

THE SONGS

This section lists, alphabetically, all titles listed in the *Top 1000* ranking. Listed next to each title is its final ranking in the *Top 1000*.

A song with more than one charted version is listed once, with the artist's names listed below it in rank order. Songs that have the same title, but are different tunes, are listed separately, with the highest ranked song listed first.

A

365 **ABC** *Jackson 5*
297 **Abracadabra** *Steve Miller Band*
657 **Addicted To Love** *Robert Palmer*
Admiral Halsey *see: Uncle Albert*
729 **Africa** *Toto*
961 **After The Love Has Gone**
Earth, Wind & Fire
392 **Afternoon Delight** *Starland Vocal Band*
197 **Against All Odds (Take A Look At Me Now)** *Phil Collins*
220 **Ain't No Mountain High Enough**
Diana Ross
295 **Ain't That A Shame** *Pat Boone*
923 **All By Myself** *Eric Carmen*
517 **All 4 Love** *Color Me Badd*
68 **All I Have To Do Is Dream**
Everly Brothers
975 **All I Wanna Do Is Make Love To You**
Heart
105 **All Night Long (All Night)**
Lionel Richie
854 **All Out Of Love** *Air Supply*
8 **All Shook Up** *Elvis Presley*
420 **All The Man That I Need**
Whitney Houston
930 **All Those Years Ago** *George Harrison*
725 **All You Need Is Love** *Beatles*
943 **Allegheny Moon** *Patti Page*
629 **Alley-Oop** *Hollywood Argyles*
227 **Alone** *Heart*
54 **Alone Again (Naturally)**
Gilbert O'Sullivan
658 **Always** *Atlantic Starr*
493 **Amanda** *Boston*
116 **American Pie - Parts I & II**
Don McLean
235 **American Woman** *Guess Who*
689 **Angie** *Rolling Stones*
764 **Angie Baby** *Helen Reddy*
448 **Annie's Song** *John Denver*
108 **Another Brick In The Wall (Part II)**
Pink Floyd
127 **Another Day In Paradise** *Phil Collins*
174 **Another One Bites The Dust** *Queen*
Another Somebody Done Somebody Wrong Song *see: (Hey Won't You Play)*
426 **Anything For You**
Gloria Estefan & Miami Sound Machine
43 **April Love** *Pat Boone*
52 **Aquarius/Let The Sunshine In**
5th Dimension
56 **Are You Lonesome To-night?**
Elvis Presley
181 **Arthur's Theme (Best That You Can Do)** *Christopher Cross*
25 **At The Hop** *Danny & The Juniors*

463 **At This Moment**
Billy Vera & The Beaters
97 **Autumn Leaves** *Roger Williams*

B

311 **Babe** *Styx*
415 **Baby Baby** *Amy Grant*
837 **Baby-Baby-Baby** *TLC*
196 **Baby Come Back** *Player*
327 **Baby, Come To Me**
Patti Austin with James Ingram
745 **Baby Don't Forget My Number**
Milli Vanilli
217 **Baby Don't Get Hooked On Me**
Mac Davis
62 **Baby Got Back** *Sir Mix-A-Lot*
732 **Baby, I Love Your Way/Freebird Medley (Free Baby)** *Will To Power*
163 **Baby Love** *Supremes*
823 **Back In My Arms Again** *Supremes*
511 **Bad** *Michael Jackson*
375 **Bad, Bad Leroy Brown** *Jim Croce*
293 **Bad Blood** *Neil Sedaka*
78 **Bad Girls** *Donna Summer*
490 **Bad Medicine** *Bon Jovi*
840 **Baker Street** *Gerry Rafferty*
94 **Ballad Of The Green Berets**
SSgt Barry Sadler
684 **Band On The Run**
Paul McCartney & Wings
787 **Batdance** *Prince*
46 **Battle Of New Orleans** *Johnny Horton*
934 **Be My Baby** *Ronettes*
194 **Beat It** *Michael Jackson*
123 **Because I Love You (The Postman Song)** *Stevie B*
605 **Before The Next Teardrop Falls**
Freddy Fender
889 **Being With You** *Smokey Robinson*
(Believe It Or Not) *see: Theme From Greatest American Hero*
710 **Ben** *Michael Jackson*
568 **Bennie And The Jets** *Elton John*
67 **Best Of My Love** *Emotions*
750 **Best Of My Love** *Eagles*
(Best That You Can Do) *see: Arthur's Theme*
9 **Bette Davis Eyes** *Kim Carnes*
84 **Big Bad John** *Jimmy Dean*
82 **Big Girls Don't Cry** *4 Seasons*
456 **Big Hunk O' Love** *Elvis Presley*
31 **Billie Jean** *Michael Jackson*
440 **Billy, Don't Be A Hero**
Bo Donaldson & The Heywoods
536 **Bird Dog** *Everly Brothers*
824 **Black & White** *Three Dog Night*
815 **Black Cat** *Janet Jackson*
34 **Black Or White** *Michael Jackson*

740 **Holding Back The Years** *Simply Red*
86 **Honey** *Bobby Goldsboro*
102 **Honeycomb** *Jimmie Rodgers*
872 **Honky Tonk** *Bill Doggett*
119 **Honky Tonk Women** *Rolling Stones*
672 **Hooked On A Feeling** *Blue Swede*
928 **Horse, The** *Cliff Nobles & Co.*
207 **Horse With No Name** *America*
553 **Hot Child In The City** *Nick Gilder*
519 **Hot Diggity (Dog Ziggity Boom)**
     Perry Como
175 **Hot Stuff** *Donna Summer*
608 **Hotel California** *Eagles*
255 **House Of The Rising Sun** *Animals*
286 **How Am I Supposed To Live Without
     You** *Michael Bolton*
130 **How Can You Mend A Broken Heart**
     Bee Gees
172 **How Deep Is Your Love** *Bee Gees*
319 **How Do You Talk To An Angel**
     Heights
462 **How Will I Know** *Whitney Houston*
651 **Human** *Human League*
847 **Hurts So Good** *John Cougar*
695 **Hustle, The** *Van McCoy*

I

428 **I Adore Mi Amor** *Color Me Badd*
100 **I Almost Lost My Mind** *Pat Boone*
613 **I Am Woman** *Helen Reddy*
494 **I Can Help** *Billy Swan*
156 **I Can See Clearly Now** *Johnny Nash*
307 **I Can't Get Next To You** *Temptations*
149 **(I Can't Get No) Satisfaction**
     Rolling Stones
528 **I Can't Go For That (No Can Do)**
     Daryl Hall & John Oates
326 **I Can't Help Myself** *Four Tops*
75 **I Can't Stop Loving You** *Ray Charles*
643 **I Don't Have The Heart** *James Ingram*
393 **I Don't Wanna Cry** *Mariah Carey*
283 **I Feel Fine** *Beatles*
354 **I Get Around** *Beach Boys*
284 **I Got You Babe** *Sonny & Cher*
950 **I Gotcha** *Joe Tex*
507 **I Hear A Symphony** *Supremes*
876 **I Hear You Knocking** *Gale Storm*
     I Heard It Through The Grapevine
32 *Marvin Gaye*
898 *Gladys Knight & The Pips*
512 **I Honestly Love You**
     Olivia Newton-John
200 **I Just Called To Say I Love You**
     Stevie Wonder
791 **I Just Can't Stop Loving You**
     Michael Jackson
485 **(I Just) Died In Your Arms**
     Cutting Crew

99 **I Just Want To Be Your Everything**
     Andy Gibb
442 **I Knew You Were Waiting (For Me)**
     Aretha Franklin & George Michael
920 **I Like It Like That** *Chris Kenner*
558 **I Like The Way (The Kissing Game)**
     Hi-Five
328 **I Love A Rainy Night** *Eddie Rabbitt*
27 **I Love Rock 'N Roll** *Joan Jett*
881 **I Love Your Smile** *Shanice*
819 **I Shot The Sheriff** *Eric Clapton*
437 **I Still Haven't Found What I'm Looking
     For** *U2*
189 **I Think I Love You** *Partridge Family*
481 **I Think We're Alone Now** *Tiffany*
346 **I Wanna Dance With Somebody (Who
     Loves Me)** *Whitney Houston*
855 **I Wanna Sex You Up** *Color Me Badd*
769 **I Want To Be Wanted** *Brenda Lee*
29 **I Want To Hold Your Hand** *Beatles*
376 **I Want To Know What Love Is**
     Foreigner
567 **I Want You Back** *Jackson 5*
521 **I Want You, I Need You, I Love You**
     Elvis Presley
1 **I Will Always Love You**
     Whitney Houston
251 **I Will Follow Him** *Little Peggy March*
177 **I Will Survive** *Gloria Gaynor*
610 **I Wish** *Stevie Wonder*
542 **I Write The Songs** *Barry Manilow*
949 **I'd Really Love To See You Tonight**
     England Dan & John Ford Coley
743 **I'll Be Loving You (Forever)**
     New Kids On The Block
     I'll Be There
72 *Jackson 5*
390 *Mariah Carey*
755 **I'll Be There For You** *Bon Jovi*
809 **I'll Be Your Everything** *Tommy Page*
621 **I'll Take You There** *Staple Singers*
30 **I'm A Believer** *Monkees*
984 **I'm Gonna Make You Love Me**
     Supremes & Temptations
799 **I'm Henry VIII, I Am** *Herman's Hermits*
925 **I'm In You** *Peter Frampton*
445 **I'm Leaving It Up To You** *Dale & Grace*
940 **I'm Not In Love** *10cc*
185 **I'm Sorry** *Brenda Lee*
827 **I'm Sorry** *John Denver*
509 **I'm Telling You Now**
     Freddie & The Dreamers
183 **I'm Too Sexy** *Right Said Fred*
618 **I'm Your Baby Tonight**
     Whitney Houston
728 **I'm Your Boogie Man**
     KC & The Sunshine Band
749 **I've Been Thinking About You**
     Londonbeat

125

MICHAEL
OF THE JACKSON 5

His own smash single!

"GOT TO BE THERE"

RECORD NO. M 1191F

Q

405 **Quarter To Three** *U.S. Bonds*
(Que Sera, Sera) *see: Whatever Will Be, Will Be*
945 **Queen Of Hearts** *Juice Newton*

R

454 **Rag Doll** *4 Seasons*
981 **Rain, The Park & Other Things**
Cowsills
104 **Raindrops Keep Fallin' On My Head**
B.J. Thomas
978 **Ramblin' Rose** *Nat King Cole*
391 **Rapture** *Blondie*
444 **Reach Out I'll Be There** *Four Tops*
727 **Red Red Wine** *UB40*
382 **Reflex, The** *Duran Duran*
421 **Release Me** *Wilson Phillips*
455 **Respect** *Aretha Franklin*
843 **Return To Sender** *Elvis Presley*
124 **Reunited** *Peaches & Herb*
330 **Rhinestone Cowboy** *Glen Campbell*
475 **Rich Girl** *Daryl Hall & John Oates*
858 **Ride Like The Wind** *Christopher Cross*
968 **Right Back Where We Started From**
Maxine Nightingale
267 **Right Here Waiting** *Richard Marx*
306 **Ring My Bell** *Anita Ward*
721 **Ringo** *Lorne Greene*
341 **Rise** *Herb Alpert*
36 **Rock And Roll Waltz** *Kay Starr*
13 **Rock Around The Clock** *Bill Haley*
271 **Rock Me Amadeus** *Falco*
761 **Rock Me Gently** *Andy Kim*
(806) **Rock On** *Michael Damian*
817 **Rock The Boat** *Hues Corporation*
135 **Rock With You** *Michael Jackson*
513 **Rock Your Baby** *George McCrae*
803 **Rock'n Me** *Steve Miller*
Rockin' Robin
946 *Bobby Day*
988 *Michael Jackson*
165 **Roll With It** *Steve Winwood*
635 **Romantic** *Karyn White*
Romeo & Juliet *see: Love Theme From*
842 **Rosanna** *Toto*
(132) **Roses Are Red (My Love)** *Bobby Vinton*
(296) **Round And Round** *Perry Como*
894 **Rubberband Man** *Spinners*
(932) **Ruby Baby** *Dion*
(724) **Ruby Tuesday** *Rolling Stones*
874 **Rump Shaker** *Wreckx-N-Effect*
364 **Runaround Sue** *Dion*
147 **Runaway** *Del Shannon*
202 **Running Bear** *Johnny Preston*
826 **Running Scared** *Roy Orbison*
87 **Rush, Rush** *Paula Abdul*

S

552 **Sad Eyes** *Robert John*
677 **Sailing** *Christopher Cross*
Saint *see: St.*
(679) **Sara** *Starship*
Satisfaction *see: (I Can't Get No)*
811 **Satisfied** *Richard Marx*
777 **Saturday Night** *Bay City Rollers*
66 **Save The Best For Last**
Vanessa Williams
(214) **Save The Last Dance For Me** *Drifters*
647 **Saving All My Love For You**
Whitney Houston
857 **Say It Isn't So** *Daryl Hall - John Oates*
45 **Say Say Say**
Paul McCartney & Michael Jackson
137 **Say You, Say Me** *Lionel Richie*
730 **Seasons Change** *Expose*
226 **Seasons In The Sun** *Terry Jacks*
564 **Separate Lives**
Phil Collins & Marilyn Martin
591 **Set Adrift On Memory Bliss** *PM Dawn*
24 **Shadow Dancing** *Andy Gibb*
Shaft *see: Theme From*
533 **(Shake, Shake, Shake) Shake Your Booty** *KC & The Sunshine Band*
596 **Shake You Down** *Gregory Abbott*
668 **Shakedown** *Bob Seger*
863 **Shame On The Moon** *Bob Seger*
926 **Shattered Dreams** *Johnny Hates Jazz*
432 **She Ain't Worth It**
Glenn Medeiros/Bobby Brown
656 **She Drives Me Crazy**
Fine Young Cannibals
(312) **She Loves You** *Beatles*
499 **Sheila** *Tommy Roe*
(95) **Sherry** *4 Seasons*
802 **Shining Star** *Earth, Wind & Fire*
938 **Short People** *Randy Newman*
268 **Shout** *Tears For Fears*
640 **Show And Tell** *Al Wilson*
73 **Silly Love Songs** *Wings*
4 **Singing The Blues** *Guy Mitchell*
239 **Sir Duke** *Stevie Wonder*
829 **Sister Golden Hair** *America*
118 **(Sittin' On) The Dock Of The Bay**
Otis Redding
971 **16 Candles** *Crests*
15 **Sixteen Tons** *Tennessee Ernie Ford*
661 **Sledgehammer** *Peter Gabriel*
(350) **Sleep Walk** *Santo & Johnny*
883 **Slow Hand** *Pointer Sisters*
(199) **Smoke Gets In Your Eyes** *Platters*
865 **Snoopy Vs. The Red Baron**
Royal Guardsmen
619 **So Emotional** *Whitney Houston*
702 **So Much In Love** *Tymes*
846 **So Rare** *Jimmy Dorsey*

131

913 **Those Were The Days** *Mary Hopkin*
128 **Three Bells** *Browns*
305 **Three Times A Lady** *Commodores*
798 **Ticket To Ride** *Beatles*
539 **Tide Is High** *Blondie*
115 **Tie A Yellow Ribbon Round The Ole Oak Tree** *Dawn*
359 **Tighten Up** *Archie Bell & The Drells*
343 **Time After Time** *Cyndi Lauper*
960 **Time (Clock Of The Heart)** *Culture Club*
(443) **Time In A Bottle** *Jim Croce*
Time Of My Life *see: (I've Had)*
208 **To Be With You** *Mr. Big*
186 **To Know Him Is To Love Him** *Teddy Bears*
88 **To Sir With Love** *Lulu*
776 **Together Forever** *Rick Astley*
527 **Tom Dooley** *Kingston Trio*
(20) **Tonight's The Night (Gonna Be Alright)** *Rod Stewart*
985 **Too Late To Turn Back Now** *Cornelius Brothers & Sister Rose*
216 **Too Much** *Elvis Presley*
337 **Too Much Heaven** *Bee Gees*
632 **Too Much, Too Little, Too Late** *Johnny Mathis/Deniece Williams*
377 **Top Of The World** *Carpenters*
317 **Torn Between Two Lovers** *Mary MacGregor*
26 **Tossin' And Turnin'** *Bobby Lewis*
114 **Total Eclipse Of The Heart** *Bonnie Tyler*
597 **Touch Me In The Morning** *Diana Ross*
482 **Toy Soldiers** *Martika*
348 **Tragedy** *Bee Gees*
386 **Travelin' Man** *Ricky Nelson*
491 **True Colors** *Cyndi Lauper*
325 **Truly** *Lionel Richie*
249 **Turn! Turn! Turn!** *Byrds*
902 **26 Miles (Santa Catalina)** *Four Preps*
(530) **Twilight Time** *Platters*
170 **Twist, The** *Chubby Checker*
866 **Twist And Shout** *Beatles*
436 **Two Hearts** *Phil Collins*
927 **Typical Male** *Tina Turner*

U

562 **Unbelievable** *EMF*
707 **Uncle Albert/Admiral Halsey** *Paul & Linda McCartney*
637 **Undercover Angel** *Alan O'Day*
260 **Up Where We Belong** *Joe Cocker & Jennifer Warnes*
101 **Upside Down** *Diana Ross*

V

Valley Of The Dolls *see: Theme From*

(81) **Venus** *Frankie Avalon*
Venus
585 *Shocking Blue*
693 *Bananarama*
487 **View To A Kill** *Duran Duran*
164 **Vision Of Love** *Mariah Carey*
225 **Vogue** *Madonna*
83 **Volare (Nel Blu Dipinto Di Blu)** *Domenico Modugno*

W

833 **Waiting For A Girl Like You** *Foreigner*
229 **Wake Me Up Before You Go-Go** *Wham!*
107 **Wake Up Little Susie** *Everly Brothers*
277 **Walk Like A Man** *4 Seasons*
154 **Walk Like An Egyptian** *Bangles*
453 **Walk Right In** *Rooftop Singers*
625 **Want Ads** *Honey Cone*
241 **War** *Edwin Starr*
602 **Way It Is** *Bruce Hornsby*
209 **Way We Were** *Barbra Streisand*
763 **Way You Make Me Feel** *Michael Jackson*
14 **Wayward Wind** *Gogi Grant*
160 **We Are The World** *USA for Africa*
418 **We Built This City** *Starship*
281 **We Can Work It Out** *Beatles*
384 **We Didn't Start The Fire** *Billy Joel*
896 **We Got The Beat** *Go-Go's*
765 **We're An American Band** *Grand Funk*
861 **We've Only Just Begun** *Carpenters*
236 **Wedding Bell Blues** *5th Dimension*
715 **Welcome Back** *John Sebastian*
662 **West End Girls** *Pet Shop Boys*
What A Feeling *see: Flashdance*
579 **What A Fool Believes** *Doobie Brothers*
(906) **What's Going On** *Marvin Gaye*
193 **What's Love Got To Do With It** *Tina Turner*
832 **Whatever Gets You Thru The Night** *John Lennon*
875 **Whatever Will Be, Will Be (Que Sera, Sera)** *Doris Day*
When A Man Loves A Woman
503 *Percy Sledge*
565 *Michael Bolton*
69 **When Doves Cry** *Prince*
663 **When I Need You** *Leo Sayer*
464 **When I See You Smile** *Bad English*
484 **When I Think Of You** *Janet Jackson*
805 **When I'm With You** *Sheriff*
362 **Where Did Our Love Go** *Supremes*
486 **Where Do Broken Hearts Go** *Whitney Houston*
555 **Who Can It Be Now?** *Men At Work*
789 **Who's That Girl** *Madonna*
586 **Why** *Frankie Avalon*

864 **Wild Boys**   *Duran Duran*
413 **Wild Thing**   *Troggs*
638 **Wild, Wild West**   *Escape Club*
388 **Will It Go Round In Circles**
       Billy Preston
422 **Will You Love Me Tomorrow**   *Shirelles*
206 **Winchester Cathedral**
       New Vaudeville Band
641 **Wind Beneath My Wings**   *Bette Midler*
145 **Windy**   *Association*
731 **Wishing Well**   *Terence Trent D'Arby*
180 **Witch Doctor**   *David Seville*
400 **With A Little Luck**   *Wings*
238 **With Or Without You**   *U2*
142 **Without You**   *Nilsson*
880 **Woman**   *John Lennon*
184 **Woman In Love**   *Barbra Streisand*
201 **Wonderland By Night**   *Bert Kaempfert*
698 **Wooden Heart**   *Joe Dowell*
958 **Wooly Bully**
       Sam The Sham & the Pharoahs
965 **Working My Way Back To You**
       (medley)   *Spinners*
634 **World Without Love**   *Peter & Gordon*

Y

878 **Y.M.C.A.**   *Village People*
575 **Yakety Yak**   *Coasters*
 38 **Yellow Rose Of Texas**   *Mitch Miller*
992 **Yes, I'm Ready**   *Teri DeSario with K.C.*
169 **Yesterday**   *Beatles*
812 **You Ain't Seen Nothing Yet**
       Bachman-Turner Overdrive
686 **You Are The Sunshine Of My Life**
       Stevie Wonder
410 **You Can't Hurry Love**   *Supremes*
321 **You Don't Bring Me Flowers**
       Barbra Streisand & Neil Diamond
590 **You Don't Have To Be A Star (To Be In**
       My Show)
       Marilyn McCoo & Billy Davis, Jr.

941 **You Don't Own Me**   *Lesley Gore*
738 **You Give Love A Bad Name**   *Bon Jovi*
666 **You Haven't Done Nothin**
       Stevie Wonder
    You Keep Me Hangin' On
504   *Supremes*
757   *Kim Wilde*
  6 **You Light Up My Life**   *Debby Boone*
970 **You Make Me Feel Brand New**
       Stylistics
595 **You Make Me Feel Like Dancing**
       Leo Sayer
592 **You Needed Me**   *Anne Murray*
178 **You Send Me**   *Sam Cooke*
692 **You Should Be Dancing**   *Bee Gees*
974 **You'll Never Find Another Love Like**
       Mine   *Lou Rawls*
291 **(You're) Having My Baby**   *Paul Anka*
667 **You're In Love**   *Wilson Phillips*
252 **(You're My) Soul And Inspiration**
       Righteous Brothers
818 **You're No Good**   *Linda Ronstadt*
699 **You're Sixteen**   *Ringo Starr*
192 **You're So Vain**   *Carly Simon*
560 **You're The One That I Want**
       John Travolta & Olivia Newton-John
631 **You've Got A Friend**   *James Taylor*
352 **You've Lost That Lovin' Feelin'**
       Righteous Brothers
933 **You've Made Me So Very Happy**
       Blood, Sweat & Tears
905 **Young Girl**
       Union Gap feat. Gary Puckett
    Young Love
 47   *Tab Hunter*
524   *Sonny James*

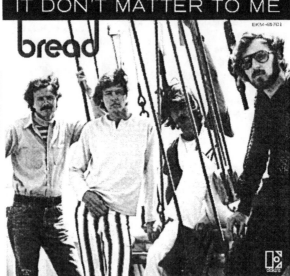

another Hit single from

bread

IT DON'T MATTER TO ME

EKM-45701

bread

"IT DON'T MATTER TO ME" EKM-45701 B/W "CALL ON ME"
PRODUCED BY DAVID GATES WITH JAMES GRIFFIN AND ROBB ROYER
FROM ELEKTRA

MISCELLANEOUS

THE TOP 50 ARTISTS OF THE *TOP 1000*

RANK	TOP 1000		RANK	TOP 1000	
1)	21	The Beatles	26)	5	Olivia Newton-John
2)	20	Elvis Presley	27)	5	Prince
3)	14	Michael Jackson	28)	5	Janet Jackson
4)	13	The Supremes	29)	5	Bon Jovi
5)	11	Paul McCartney/Wings	30)	5	The Temptations
6)	11	Madonna	31)	5	Carpenters
7)	10	George Michael/Wham!	32)	5	Eagles
8)	10	Whitney Houston	33)	5	John Denver
9)	10	Stevie Wonder	34)	4	The Platters
10)	10	The Rolling Stones	35)	4	Bobby Vinton
11)	9	Bee Gees	36)	4	Blondie
12)	8	Elton John	37)	4	Marvin Gaye
13)	8	Phil Collins	38)	4	Paul Anka
14)	7	Daryl Hall & John Oates	39)	4	Roberta Flack
15)	7	KC And The Sunshine Band	40)	4	The Beach Boys
16)	6	Pat Boone	41)	4	George Harrison
17)	6	Lionel Richie	42)	4	Connie Francis
18)	6	Mariah Carey	43)	4	Roxette
19)	6	Diana Ross	44)	4	Neil Diamond
20)	6	Paula Abdul	45)	3	Rod Stewart
21)	6	Donna Summer	46)	3	Andy Gibb
22)	6	The Jackson 5	47)	3	Dawn/Tony Orlando
23)	5	The 4 Seasons	48)	3	The Monkees
24)	5	Barbra Streisand	49)	3	Sly & The Family Stone
25)	5	The Everly Brothers	50)	3	Simon & Garfunkel

Top 1000: Artist's total records making the *Top 1000*.

For artists with the same number of *Top 1000* hits, ties are broken by totaling the final ranking of each *Top 1000* hit by these artists, and the artist with the highest ranking is listed first, and so on.

SONGS WITH MORE THAN ONE HIT VERSION
Peak Position/Year (*Top 1000* Rank)

1. **I'll Be There**
   Jackson 5   1/'70 (72)
   Mariah Carey   1/'92 (390)

2. **Young Love**
   Tab Hunter   1/'57 (47)
   Sonny James   1/'57 (524)

3. **Go Away Little Girl**
   Donny Osmond   1/'71 (218)
   Steve Lawrence   1/'63 (363)

4. **Butterfly**
   Andy Williams   1/'57 (204)
   Charlie Gracie   1/'57 (394)

5. **Lean On Me**
   Bill Withers   1/'72 (264)
   Club Nouveau   1/'87 (495)

6. **I Heard It Through The Grapevine**
   Marvin Gaye   1/'68 (32)
   Gladys Knight & The Pips   2/'67 (898)

7. **When A Man Loves A Woman**
   Percy Sledge   1/'66 (503)
   Michael Bolton   1/'91 (565)

8. **The Loco-Motion**
   Grand Funk   1/'74 (472)
   Little Eva   1/'62 (697)

9. **You Keep Me Hangin' On**
   The Supremes   1/'66 (504)
   Kim Wilde   1/'87 (757)

10. **Venus**
    The Shocking Blue   1/'70 (585)
    Bananarama   1/'86 (693)

11. **Please Mr. Postman**
    The Marvelettes   1/'61 (645)
    Carpenters   1/'75 (813)

12. **Rockin' Robin**
    Bobby Day   2/'58 (946)
    Michael Jackson   2/'72 (988)

SAME TITLES — DIFFERENT SONGS

The following *Top 1000* songs have the same title, but are not by the same composer(s). The artist with the highest ranked version is listed first, along with the year the record peaked.

Best Of My Love
   Emotions ('77)
   The Eagles ('75)

Cherish
   The Association ('66)
   Kool & The Gang ('85)

Fire
   Ohio Players ('75)
   Pointer Sisters ('79)

Good Vibrations
   Beach Boys ('66)
   Marky Mark & The
      Funky Bunch ('91)

Heaven
   Bryan Adams ('85)
   Warrant ('89)

I'm Sorry
   Brenda Lee ('60)
   John Denver ('75)

Jump
   Van Halen ('84)
   Kris Kross ('92)

My Love
   Paul McCartney & Wings ('73)
   Petula Clark ('66)

One More Try
   George Michael ('88)
   Timmy -T- ('91)

Venus
   Frankie Avalon ('59)
   The Shocking Blue ('70) and
      Bananarama ('86)

137

RE-CHARTED SINGLES

The *Top 1000* singles which hit the charts more than once.

RANK	Peak Position/Year(Weeks Charted)
13)	**Rock Around The Clock**...*Bill Haley & His Comets* 1/'55(24); 39/'74(14)
14)	**The Wayward Wind**...*Gogi Grant* 1/'56(28); 50/'61(9)
68)	**All I Have To Do Is Dream**...*The Everly Brothers* 1/'58(17); 96/'61(2)
134)	**Daydream Believer**...*The Monkees* 1/'67(12); 79/'86(4)
146)	**Ode To Billie Joe**...*Bobbie Gentry* 1/'67(14); 54/'76(6)
168)	**The Chipmunk Song**...*The Chipmunks* 1/'58(13); 41/'59(5); 45/'60(3); 39/'61(3); 40/'62(4)
170)	**The Twist**...*Chubby Checker* 1/'60(18); 1/'62(21)
213)	**Light My Fire**...*The Doors* 1/'67(17); 87/'68(6)
372)	**Monster Mash**...*Bobby "Boris" Pickett & The Crypt-Kickers* 1/'62(14); 91/'70(3); 10/'73(20)
463)	**At This Moment**...*Billy Vera & The Beaters* 79/'81(3); 1/'87(21)
512)	**I Honestly Love You**...*Olivia Newton-John* 1/'74(15); 48/'77(9)
727)	**Red Red Wine**...*UB40* 34/'84(15); 1/'88(25)
805)	**When I'm With You**...*Sheriff* 61/'83(7); 1/'89(21)
841)	**Louie Louie**...*The Kingsmen* 2/'63(16); 97/'66(2)
866)	**Twist And Shout**...*The Beatles* 2/'64(11); 23/'86(15)
872)	**Honky Tonk**...*Bill Doggett* 2/'56(29); 57/'61(10)

138

BREAKDOWN BY YEAR

Total records making the *Top 1000* year-by-year.

YR	TOP 1000		YR	TOP 1000
55	9		70	23
56	22		71	22
57	25		72	27
58	28		73	31
59	21		74	38
Total	105 (10.5%)		75	37
			76	35
			77	33
			78	22
			79	27
			Total	295 (29.5%)

YR	TOP 1000		YR	TOP 1000
60	23		80	21
61	24		81	26
62	23		82	21
63	25		83	23
64	25		84	23
65	27		85	29
66	30		86	34
67	25		87	32
68	21		88	33
69	23		89	35
Total	246 (24.6%)		Total	277 (27.7%)

YR	TOP 1000
90	28
91	30
92	19
Total	77 (7.7%)

JOEL WHITBURN:
CHARTING HIS OWN COURSE

It was in 1970 that Joel Whitburn published the book bound to become a business. The book — *Top Pop Records* — was a natural outgrowth of Joel's love of records and his penchant for filling file cards with *Billboard* chart data on each record he owned, the better to control his swelling collection.

This slim, 104-page volume — listing every single to ever appear on *Billboard's* Pop music charts from 1955-1969 — was soon a big hit with the record and radio industries. And Record Research Inc. was born.

Since then, few, if any, individuals have taken the charts to heart quite like Joel Whitburn. In addition to *Top 1000 Singles* 1955-1993, "the world's foremost chart authority" has compiled well over thirty other books detailing the history and development of charted music from 1890 to the present.

Today, Joel's team of Record Researchers delves deeper into *Billboard's* charts than every before, pouring out a steady stream of chart reference books widely noted for their detail, diversity, and painstaking accuracy. These books, currently used worldwide by collectors, disc jockeys, program directors, musicologists, artists and others, cover musical genres ranging from pop to country to R&B and beyond.

As the largest privately-held record collection in the world, Joel's vast music library completely fills an environmentally-controlled underground vault adjacent to his Menomonee Falls, Wisconsin home. Here you'll find all the 100,000+ titles that ever appeared on *Billboard's* "Hot 100" and "Top Pop Albums" charts, along with a good share of the records that made *Billboard's* other charts.

And here, too, you'll find Joel Whitburn, collector extraordinaire, for whom charting a record's rise and fall has never lost its excitement or intrigue.

ALL THE HITS THAT

Only Joel Whitburn's Record Research Books List Every

When the talk turns to music, more people turn to Joel Whitburn's Record Research Collection than to any other reference source.

That's because these are the only books that get right to the bottom of *Billboard's* major charts, with **complete, fully accurate chart data on every record ever charted.** So they're quoted with confidence by DJ's, music show hosts, program directors, collectors and other music enthusiasts worldwide.

Each book lists every record's significant chart data, such as peak position, debut date, peak date, weeks charted, label, record number and much more, all conveniently arranged for fast, easy reference. Most books also feature artist biographies, record notes, RIAA Platinum/Gold Record certifications, top artist and record achievements, all-time artist and record rankings, a chronological listing of all #1 hits, and additional in-depth chart information.

And now, the new large-format **Billboard Hot 100/Pop Singles Charts** book series takes chart research one step further, by actually reproducing weekly pop singles charts by decade.

Joel Whitburn's Record Research Collection. #1 on **everyone's** hit list.

TOP POP SINGLES 1955-1990
Nearly 20,000 Pop singles - every "Hot 100" hit - arranged by artist. 848 pages. Softcover. $60.

POP SINGLES ANNUAL 1955-1990
A year-by-year ranking, based on chart performance, of the nearly 20,000 Pop hits. 736 pages. $70 Hardcover/$60 Softcover.

TOP POP ALBUMS 1955-1992
An artist-by-artist history of the over 17,000 LPs that ever appeared on *Billboard's* Pop albums charts, with a complete A-Z listing below each artist of every track from every charted album by that artist. 976 pages. Hardcover. $95.

TOP POP ALBUM TRACKS 1955-1992
An all-inclusive, alphabetical index of every song track from every charted music album, with the artist's name and the album's chart debut year. 544 pages. Hardcover. $55.

THE BILLBOARD HOT 100/POP SINGLES CHARTS:

THE EIGHTIES 1980-1989
THE SEVENTIES 1970-1979
THE SIXTIES 1960-1969
POP CHARTS 1955-1959
Three complete collections of the actual weekly "Hot 100" charts from each decade, reproduced in black-and-white at 70% of original size. Over 550 pages each. Deluxe Hardcover. $95 each. Reproductions of every weekly Pop singles chart *Billboard* published from 1955 through 1959 ("Best Sellers," "Jockeys," "Juke Box," "Top 100" and "Hot 100"). 496 pages. Deluxe Hardcover. $95.

POP MEMORIES 1890-1954
The only documented chart history of early American popular music, arranged by artist. 660 pages. Hardcover. $60.

TOP COUNTRY SINGLES 1944-1988
An artist-by-artist listing of every "Country" single ever charted. 564 pages. $60 Hardcover/$50 Softcover.

EVER CHARTED!

Record To Ever Appear On Every Major *Billboard* Chart.

TOP R&B SINGLES 1942-1988
Every "Soul," "Black," "Urban Contemporary" and "Rhythm & Blues" charted single, listed by artist. 624 pages. $60 Hardcover/$50 Softcover.

BILLBOARD'S TOP 10 CHARTS 1958-1988
1,550 actual, weekly Top 10 Pop singles charts in the original "Hot 100" chart format. 600 pages. Softcover. $50.

BUBBLING UNDER THE HOT 100 1959-1985
The complete history of *Billboard's* Bubbling Under chart, listed by artist. Also features Bubbling Under titles that later hit the "Hot 100." 384 pages. Hardcover. $45.

BILLBOARD #1s 1950-1991
A week-by-week listing of every #1 single and album from *Billboard's* Pop, R&B, Country and Adult Contemporary charts. 336 pages. Softcover. $35.

DAILY #1 HITS 1940-1992
A desktop calendar of a half-century of #1 pop records. Lists one day of the year per page of every record that held the #1 position on the Pop singles charts on that day for each of the past 53 years. 392 pages. Spiral-bound softcover. $30.

MUSIC YEARBOOKS 1983/1984/1985/1986
The complete story of each year in music, covering *Billboard's* biggest singles and albums charts. Various page lengths. Softcover. $35 each.

MUSIC & VIDEO YEARBOOKS
1987/1988/1989/1990/1991/1992
Comprehensive, yearly updates on *Billboard's* major singles, albums and videocassettes charts. Various page lengths. Softcover. $40 each.

Soon To Be Released!

BILLBOARD POP ALBUM CHARTS 1965-1969
The greatest of all album eras ... straight off the pages of *Billboard!* Every weekly *Billboard* Pop albums chart, shown in its entirety, from 1965 through 1969. All charts reproduced in black-and-white at 70% of original size. Over 485 pages. Deluxe Hardcover. $95.

BILLBOARD TOP 1000 x 5
Here for the first time ever, are five complete separate rankings — from #1 right down through #1000 — of the all-time top charted hits of Pop Music 1940-1955, Pop Music 1955-1993, Country Music 1944-1993, R&B Music 1942-1993, and Adult Contemporary Music 1961-1993. Over 250 pages. Softcover. $30.

For complete book descriptions and ordering information, call, write or fax today.

The World's Leading Authority
On Recorded Entertainment

RECORD RESEARCH INC.
P.O. Box 200
Menomonee Falls, WI 53052-0200
Phone 414-251-5408
Fax 414-251-9452

"ANNIE'S SONG"
APBO-0295
THE NEW SINGLE FROM THE HOTTEST PERFORMER IN THE BUSINESS TODAY.
MANAGEMENT THREE, LTD.
Jerry Weintraub
FROM JOHN DENVER'S UPCOMING ALBUM, "BACK HOME AGAIN."
Produced by Milt Okun
CPL1/CPS1/CPK1-0548
RCA Records and Tapes

841044